RATIONING HEALTH CARE

RATIONING HEALTH CARE

MICHAEL H COOPER

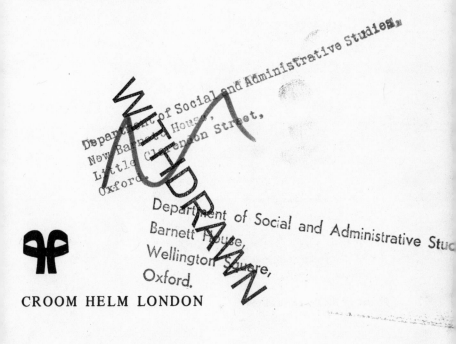

CROOM HELM LONDON

First published 1975
© 1975 by Michael H. Cooper

Reprinted 1975

Croom Helm Limited
2-10 St John's Road
London SW 11

ISBN: 0−85664−216−9

Printed by Biddles of Guildford

CONTENTS

In loving memory of my
father
Robert John Cooper

PREFACE

This book is basically a development of the ideas contained in a paper delivered to the International Economics Association meeting on the 'Economics of Health and Medical Care' held in Tokyo in April 1973. It has accordingly benefited from the discussions which took place at that meeting and from the subsequent comments of friends and colleagues. In particular I have received valuable observations and suggestions from David Stafford, Dr R.S. Inch, Professor W.J.H. Butterfield and Professor David Walker. My main debts are to Tony Culyer, Professor Dennis Lees and George Teeling-Smith who over the years have greatly added to my better understanding of socioeconomic health affairs. I thank them all most warmly whilst totally absolving them from any responsibility for the analysis and opinions which follow. Finally I should like to thank my wife and daughters for all their encouragement and numerous cups of tea which saw me through the drafting stage of this endeavour.

M.H.C.

September 1974

1 INTRODUCTION

By any set of criteria the British National Health Service is a major enterprise and yet, despite its twenty-six years of existence, there exists to date no major overall economic review of its nature and problems. The NHS currently costs the nation over £3,000m. a year (5½ per cent of the gross national product and ten per cent of public spending) and it employs over 900,000 people (five per cent of the work force). In any one year we can each expect on average to consult our general practitioner four times (representing on aggregate about thirty consultations per day per doctor) and make one visit to hospital outpatients. Over a lifetime we spend on average eight spells in hospital of approximately three and a half weeks duration each.

Further, by the very nature of its ill-defined and illusive product, the industry presents special and highly intriguing problems. The basic intention of the National Health Service Act 1946 was to establish access to health care resources for all those in need as a 'human right.' Health care resources were to be no longer rationed amongst competing claims by the ability or otherwise to pay a market price. This human right was to be made a reality as the result of the nationalisation of all health care resources and their subsequent allocation at zero or near zero prices at the point of consumption. Nationalisation was to ensure that sufficient resources were made available to meet all genuine need and, further, that they were made available efficiently and rationally. Zero prices would ensure that no one in need was deterred from demanding attention. In short, health care would become truly a social responsibility paid for by the Exchequer and equally available to all.

The need for health care was seen as finite and quantifiable. Once established, the medical profession would be charged with the task of actually determining need in individual cases and preventing the abuse of the system by those not genuinely in need. Public opinion through the ballot box would ensure adequate total provision but, within that

8

overall constraint, doctors were guaranteed complete clinical freedom to treat each and every patient as they saw fit.

In an important and fundamental sense the story of the NHS is one of success. To a very great extent financial worry has been taken out of sickness. Bankruptcy is not the inevitable outcome of major acute or chronic illness. If private practice is any barometer of success the NHS scores heavily. On the appointed day (5 July 1948) private practice shrank from being the normal form of medicine for over fifty per cent of the population to less than four per cent. Although this four per cent has persisted over the years, it has shown little sign of any marked tendency to increase. There are currently about 2¼ million people covered by private medical insurance schemes and although the revenue of these schemes has doubled over the past five years to £27m., this is largely due to higher premium levels plus the growth of group plans (particularly those paid for by employers).

The principle of zero prices has been breached many times but nevertheless direct charges to the patient still make up only some five per cent of finances, eighty-six per cent coming direct from the Exchequer and Local Authorities and nine per cent from the health component of the weekly national insurance contribution. It is the smallness of direct charges to the patient plus the system's universal coverage which, more than anything else, gives the NHS its claim to uniqueness. No other system in the world has such a heavy dependence upon the Exchequer and so few financial barriers between the individual in need and access to treatment and advice.

The fundamental success of the NHS is almost universally acknowledged and its performance compares favourably with that of other countries and their health care delivery systems. Many of the hopes and aspirations of its founders, however, have in practice proved to be either unobtainable or based upon false premises. Expenditure upon health care has proved anything but a self-eliminating expense. Need as assessed by medical practitioners is not finite. Further, even in the relatively rare instances in which the profession has formed a consensus view as to adequacy, such levels of provision have proved in practice to be inconsistent with competing claims upon national resources. Exercises reported elsewhere have shown that the total cost

9

of achieving even the main goals of different social agencies can amount to many times a country's total national income (Dror, 1968).

Although the NHS has proved popular with the population at large (PEP, 1961; Forsyth, 1967) the staff who have worked in it have forecast its imminent collapse almost annually. In the words of Enoch Powell 'one of the most striking features of the NHS is the continual, deafening chorus of complaint which rises day and night from every part of it' (Powell, 1966). Doctors, nurses and other professional groups have found themselves in the front line of a system which seemingly could not deliver what it had promised. Having set out to provide the impossible, namely the elimination of unmet need, the professions have found themselves increasingly fulfilling the role of assessing relative needs and rationing scarce health resources amongst them. It is with the need for this rationing and the methods by which it takes place, that economics is concerned.

The aim of this book is primarily diagnostic rather than prescriptive although in practice these are frequently inseparable. It is only from accurate diagnosis that sensible blue-prints for change are likely to flow. The following three Chapters are concerned with the variables which influence and determine the demand for and the supply of, health care resources. Chapters 5 and 6 discuss rationing in both theory and practice whilst subsequent chapters discuss management and planning problems, and, finally, some probable future trends in health care provision. Although this book is primarily about the NHS, most, if not all, of the problems discussed are common to all health care delivery systems in the developed world.

2 DEMAND

At the micro level the demand process begins with an individual's own
assessment of his health state, that is, with his 'want' for better health.
In practice the scope for an individual to regard himself as unwell, and
in want, seems to be almost without limit. The survey of sickness
carried out between 1943 and 1951 revealed that seventy-five per cent
of persons questioned claimed to have suffered from ill health during
the preceding month (Logan and Brooke, 1957). More recently, two
studies have achieved strikingly similar results. Wadsworth and his
colleagues (1971) found that ninety-five per cent of those surveyed in
Bermondsey and Southwark considered themselves unwell during the
fourteen days prior to questioning whilst Dunnell and Cartwright
(1972) found only five per cent completely free of symptoms and
nine per cent claiming to have suffered from more than six different
symptoms over a similar period. About thirty per cent of the population surveyed by Dunnell and Cartwright reported suffering from
coughs and catarrh, twenty-nine per cent from 'aches and pains' and
twenty-one per cent had 'headaches.' Wadsworth reported that twenty-
six per cent of the symptoms found were consistent with respiratory
disease, twenty-one per cent with mental and emotional problems and
fifteen per cent were rheumatic aches and pains.

In the USA, Roghmann and Haggerty (1972) found that during a
twenty-eight day survey period, adults in Rochester (New York)
claimed to have been suffering from at least one disorder on over
twenty per cent of the days in question. Further, no less than forty-six
per cent of the US draft were being rejected on genuine medical
grounds (OHE, 1971). Clearly to feel unwell is perfectly normal.

If an individual decides that he is in want, he then has to decide
whether to convert his 'want' into a 'demand' by presenting himself
to some medical agency for care and advice. 'Demand' is simply an
expressed want. Fortunately for the taxpayer not all health wants find

11

expression in visits to the doctor. John Fry (1973) has estimated on the basis of a range of studies that some sixteen per cent of all symptoms probably result in no action at all, sixty-three per cent in some attempt at self-care and only twenty per cent in a visit to a general practitioner. Elliott-Binns (1973) found that the vast majority of his patients had attempted at least some kind of self-care before consulting him. Further, some thirty per cent of all drug sales by value bypass the doctor, the individual going direct to the retail chemist for 'over-the-counter' remedies. Both the Wadsworth and the Dunnell studies found that the consumption of nonprescription drugs was more than twice as frequent as those obtained on prescription from the doctor. Whether these attempts at self-care are for the more trivial disorders, however, remains an open question. In both studies, forty per cent of the drugs taken were analgesics. Rather strikingly, Dunnell found that forty per cent of all adults had taken some form of medication every day for the fourteen days of the survey period, while twenty-five per cent of them were still taking a drug originally prescribed by a doctor more than a year before.

Again, not all of the demands made on doctors can be classified as *health* wants. Individuals may go to the doctor with social problems because he is there, available and free. The lonely, for example, often go to their doctor in default of any other agency to turn to. Individuals consult their doctors to legitimise absence from school or work, to obtain state sickness benefit certificates, to gain arbitration on the need for an abortion, to obtain advice on the behaviour patterns of their wayward children or simply to get the back of their passport photographs signed. K.B. Thomas (1974) found that of 5,409 consultations over one year no fewer than 1,561 (twenty-eight per cent) were for 'services' other than the treatment of illness.

Not all health wants find any expression at all. Individuals may view themselves as sick but deliberately decide to take no action. Apart from simply judging that their condition is too trivial to merit any action, they may fear the discovery of an appalling disorder or consider that little could be done in any case to cure or relieve their condition. Quite serious disorders can be 'lived with' by a combination of self treatment and a change of life style. Research has revealed a considerable 'iceberg' of sickness which clearly would merit treatment if it ever reached a medical agency or was correctly diagnosed.

Multiple screening of the general public, carried out under the auspices of Medical Officers of Health within the Local Government Service, has revealed the extent of the 'iceberg' problem. One in six people screened in the Rotherham survey of 1965 was suffering from one to nine serious illnesses. In Southwark three years later only sixty-seven out of one thousand people were found to be completely fit and fifty per cent were referred to their family doctors. For every case of diabetes, rheumatism or epilepsy known to the general practitioner there appears to be another case undiagnosed. In the case of psychiatric illnesses, bronchitis, blood pressure, glaucoma and urinary infections there are likely to be another five cases undiscovered, whilst the untreated cases of anaemia probably exceed the treated eightfold (Israel and Teeling-Smith, 1967; Brown, 1973). Again a survey in 1968 found that ninety per cent of nondenture wearers in Darlington and Salisbury needed dental treatment. Over seventy per cent needed periodental treatment (for inflammation of the gum leading to the loss of teeth) whilst seventy-five per cent had decayed teeth. Nonetheless forty per cent considered that they required no treatment at all (Bulman, 1968). Such statistics raise many complex problems. The very definition of illness (e.g. diabetes) may change as a consequence of the knowledge gained from such surveys.

The average general practitioner may miss serious disorders simply because the vast bulk of his work is concerned with the relatively trivial. Various surveys suggest that probably twenty per cent of the requests for treatment stem from the common cold or cough. Thomas (1974) found that of the seventy-two per cent of his consultations that were for reasons of illness, in forty-three per cent he was unable to make any definite diagnosis. Given no more than reassurance, and possibly a placebo, in a follow up the bulk of these patients stated that they had been made to feel better, whilst the eleven per cent who felt no better failed to return for further treatment. Other studies show between thirty per cent and seventy-five per cent of consultations are with patients displaying no objective evidence (either psychological or physical) for their attendance (Royal College of General

Practitioners, 1958). Thus the very serious ailment can present itself only rarely to the general practitioner. He is likely to see only one cervical cancer in three years practice and only one brain tumour in ten years. Basically, however, many serious ailments fail to reach the doctor at all. People are ignorant of the workings of their own bodies and often unable to recognise warning symptoms. It is interesting to speculate on how many, in practice, can use and interpret a simple thermometer with any degree of confidence and accuracy.

The factors which determine whether an individual consults a doctor are highly complex and far from fully understood (Robinson, 1971). Kessel and Shepherd (1965), for example, rather disturbingly discovered little obvious medical difference between patients who, over a ten year period, never saw their doctors and those with the average number of attendances. Job satisfaction seems to play a large part. According to the General Household Survey (1973) the unskilled manual worker is off sick over four and a half as many days as the professionally employed and over two and a half times as much as managers and employers. Those expressing satisfaction with their jobs had almost half the number days away from work (Table 1).

TABLE 1   Days off work per person per year and work satisfaction

	Males	Females	Total
Very or fairly satisfied	7.8	6.4	7.3
Neither	9.3	6.2	8.3
Rather or very dissatisfied	13.1	18.3	13.1
Total	8.1	6.9	7.7

Source: General Household Survey, *Introductory Report*, HMSO 1973.

Marital status, family stability, personality traits and class have all been shown to affect consultation rates (Taylor, 1968; Shuval, 1972; OHE, 1972). Spinsters, widows and divorcees not only see the doctor more often but in the 65 to 74 year age bracket stay in hospital on average ninety-four days as against thirty-five days (Pulse, 1974). Similarly in Scotland where hospital admissions are classified by class, the unskilled worker has proportionally higher numbers of episodes and longer duration of stay per episode. Cartwright (1967) has shown that the working class also consult their general practitioner more frequently and for different reasons. The 'working class' consultation has a higher 'service' component (e.g. for a national insurance certificate) whereas the middle class consult rather more for non life-threatening disorders such as migraine or for forms of neuroses.

TABLE 2 Working males aged 15 or over by socioeconomic group: average number of work days lost per person per year. (England and Wales 1971)

Socioeconomic group	days lost per person per year
Professional	3.9
Employers and managers	7.2
Intermediate and junior nonmanual	6.7
Skilled manual (including foremen and supervisors) and own account non-professional	9.3
Semi-skilled manual	11.5
Unskilled manual	18.4
Total	9.1

Source: The General Household Survey *Introductory Report*. Table 8.26.

The threshold at which medical attention is sought is undoubtedly partly learned from parents and from the reception received from the doctor and his receptionist in the past. A large number of consultations are doctor determined in that a direct invitation is made to report back after a suitable lapse of time or upon the re-emergence of stated symptoms. There are also real costs involved in converting a want into a demand even within the NHS. Deterrents include the necessary expenditure of time and energy, inconvenience, travel costs, leisure foregone, the discomforts of the doctor's waiting room (which are often considerable) plus such factors as concern not to add to an already overworked doctor's load. By far the most important determinant of demand, however, is the sheer availability of resources. The knowledge that there are queues will obviously deter many would-be patients from demanding care. In the long run demand will always gravitate towards whatever level of provision there happens to be. If a visit to the doctor involves a five minute wait I am more likely to take my attack of flu to him than if it involves a wait of anything up to two hours.

At the macro level there is a large number of variables likely to affect the overall level of aggregate demand. There is, for example, considerable evidence that thresholds of tolerance are lowering through time. The certificated reasons for absence from work, for example, are becoming increasingly trivial, particularly within the lower age groups. Further, the young are showing the biggest increases in new spells of sickness. If influenza is excluded from the figures (otherwise epidemics tend to obscure any trends) the days on incapacity per person (standardised rates) between 1958 and 1969 increased by twenty-six per cent for men and eleven per cent for women. New spells of incapacity per hundred people increased by forty-four per cent for men and forty-five per cent for women. For males under thirty years, however, the increase was over sixty per cent. New spells per claimant increased for men from 1.36 to 1.51 and for women from 1.32 to 1.50. Around four per cent of men and women had more than three spells in 1969. Finally the biggest increases in spells of sickness were for the short duration illnesses (four days or less) which increased over one hundred per cent.

Sickness certificates are very unreliable indicators of morbidity as the diagnosis stated on the form often tends to a medical euphemism rather than a clinical opinion. A symptom (e.g. 'headaches') rather

TABLE 3 Spells of sickness absence and working days lost among insured population. Great Britain 1954-71.

Year (ending June)	Spells Commencing (thousands)	Days Lost (millions)
1954	6569.1	280.64
1955	7037.1	276.77
1956	7183.9	275.28
1957	6669.4	262.42
1958	9404.0	292.38
1959	8035.3	282.49
1960	7496.1	274.93
1961	8257.6	278.95
1962	8504.0	280.00
1963	8444.5	288.86
1964	8128.0	286.95
1965	8751.0	299.24
1966	9533.5	311.47
1967	8640.2	301.13
1968	9770.4	327.58
1969	9784.9	329.39
1970	10596.9	342.07
1971	8613.5	314.13

Note: Number of days lost are calculated on the assumption of a six day working week.

Source: DHSS.

than an illness is often stated. Such data, of course, exclude all short absences from work, most married women and anyone not of working age. Further, periods of absence probably reflect the generosity of current sickness benefits as much as thresholds of sickness. In 1969 a married man with two children, earning £25 a week, received seventy per cent of his normal pay when off sick two weeks or more, but in 1960 with a comparable wage of £14 a week he would have received only forty per cent (Whitehead, 1971). Whatever the reasons, however, there is little doubt that increases in benefits bring large increases in claims and that claims are for increasingly vague and ill defined health states.

The Royal College of General Practitioners, surveys of morbidity lend further support to these trends (D.L. Crombie, 1974). Comparing morbidity in 1955-56 with that in 1970-71 reveals an increase in episodes of illness presented to the general practitioner but a decrease in the number of consultations per episode. Further, whilst both the number of persons failing to consult the doctor at all and the number of recorded episodes of very serious ailments have remained constant, virtually all other ailments show an increase except for skin and stomach disorders.

One of the most important factors influencing the overall demand for health care is, of course, changes in the population at risk. The distribution of demand for medical services by age is 'U'-shaped, with the young and old making by far the greatest demands. Since the inception of the NHS, the elderly (defined as males over sixty-five years old and females over sixty) have increased from 6.9m. to 9.1m. or from 13.6 per cent to 16.3 per cent of the total population. In 1971-2 although only sixteen per cent of the population at risk, they were responsible for twenty-eight per cent of all NHS expenditure (Wroe, 1973). The elderly make particularly heavy demands on the hospital system. Those aged seventy-five or over account for twenty-nine per cent of all bed use after excluding psychiatric and maternity cases. On the same basis, women alone account for twenty per cent, and all those over sixty-five years old for forty-eight per cent of average daily bed use. Furthermore, the utilisation of all hospital beds by people aged sixty-five or over increased by over thirty per cent between 1957 and 1970 due to a combination of increasing numbers and increasing referral rates. Again, twenty-five per cent of all pre-scriptions are for persons aged sixty-five or more, and general practitioners are paid an extra capitation fee of £2.10 in respect of them. According to the General Household Survey, the consultation rate for those over seventy-five was 7.3 compared with 3.6 for those aged fifteen to forty-four years.

Population projections to the year 2001 suggest no change in the numbers of elderly aged under seventy-five years but an increase of thirty-five per cent in those over seventy-five. The nation will, therefore, increasingly be faced with the pyramid problem of degenerative disorders. Further, the current old have only modest expectations of the health service but as the contemporary young get older and eventually retire, they are likely to make much greater *per capita* demands upon the system (Eardley and Wakefield, 1974).

Since the inception of the NHS there has also been a marked increase in orientation towards, and awareness of, health matters in general. Television and magazines have made the public increasingly aware of the health dangers of neglecting symptoms and also of what is technologically possible. Most women's magazines appear almost obsessed with health (and sexual) problems. Further, the media have helped to advertise the dangers associated with smoking, drinking to excess, obesity, promiscuity, drug addiction and, probably the most understated problem of them all, lack of exercise. Life styles clearly affect the demands made on the NHS very significantly. Studies have shown, for example, that both the number of spells of sickness and the duration of each are greater for the single, widowed and divorced than for the married (Wroe, 1973; Ashford and Pearson, 1970).

In addition to the factors mentioned above there are the effects on health of pollution, urbanisation, the emergence of new disorders and so on. Overall the picture is of a large and expanding demand for health care resources. In theory the scope for demand to grow is virtually limitless. The NHS, however, is not concerned with demand as such but with 'need.'

3 NEED

'Needs' are those demands which in the opinion of the doctor require medical attention. That is, they are an expert's view of our health state. The 1973 White Paper on Expenditure states the objective of the NHS to be 'to meet health needs wherever and whenever they arise.' Unfortunately, need, like beauty, is in the eye of the beholder. It is a medical opinion and not a medical fact, one of many possible points along a continuum and likely to differ widely from doctor to doctor and from moment to moment. What levels, for example, of blood sugar or emotional stress are abnormal are not matters likely to attract medical unanimity readily. It is likely to be only those conditions at the extreme ends of the continuum, where life is unambiguously threatened by inaction, that will be accepted universally as 'need.'

Once the doctor is faced by a patient, he has the choice of treating, referring to a consultant or doing nothing. Again the decision-making process is complex and little understood. There is little doubt that besides the patient's physical and mental state, his education, class, manners and sheer persistence will play a significant part. Certainly in any case the dice are heavily loaded against the doctor deciding to do nothing. At the very least a placebo will be prescribed. If the patient expresses a 'want' it is difficult for the doctor to be sure that he is mistaken, still less to accuse the patient of being a malingerer. Further, the layman has the deep-seated conviction that medicine can always, if not cure, then at least help and the profession has never been anxious to advertise its limitations. As medical science enjoys roughly the same degree of exactitude as economics (and scarcely more unanimity of opinion) the patient who is insistent is bound to use up considerable quantities of scarce resources. The doctor makes his decisions about need in face to face confrontations with patients anxious to be helped and he is, in turn, anxious not to appear helpless.

The scope for individual medical interpretation of need is well illustrated by the facility with which numbers of British dockers, until recently considered fit, have managed to find doctors who genuinely consider them unfit and therefore eligible for redundancy from the docks and for the consequential 'golden handshake.' Similarly, a leading professional footballer in 1973 upon attempting to change club was found to be suffering from a 'serious' congenital heart disorder. He continues to play football for his old club unimpaired by his newly discovered state of health.

Need can often be a matter of fashion. Some years ago the US Child Health Association surveyed one thousand eleven-year old children. Sixty-one per cent were found to have had their tonsils removed. The remaining thirty-nine per cent were referred to doctors for medical examination. Tonsilectomy was promptly recommended for forty-five per cent of them. The remaining fifty-five per cent were again referred to a different set of doctors and a further forty-four per cent of these were told they 'needed' their tonsils removed. After three examinations, only sixty-five children (6.5 per cent) had not had a tonsilectomy recommended (Malleson, 1973).

One of the most striking areas of doubt is the field of mental health. Rosenham (1973) at Stanford recently managed to plant eight 'normal' people in mental hospitals where they remained undetected for as long as they could endure it. Further, within a mental hospital warned of impending planted normal patients, one consultant detected forty-one and another twenty-three out of a population of 193 entirely 'genuine' patients already diagnosed elsewhere as being mentally sick. Perhaps the best illustration of the scope for variations in need assessment is the contrast between American and British surgery rates. Hospital surgeons in the USA manage to find twice as many patients *per capita* in need of surgery as do their British counterparts. This contrast is made all the more surprising by the existence of a large medically deprived population in the USA and by the existence of large numbers of operations outside of hospital there. It has been suggested that it is the lure of extra fees in the USA which accounts for the discrepancy but if the American system has an inbuilt incentive to work maximise, then equally the British salaried system has an incentive to work

21

minimise. Caldwell Esselstyn is quoted as saying that the medical profession is not sufficiently mature to resist the temptation of unnecessary procedures inherent in a fee-per-item of service system. If this is true it equally invites the question as to whether it is mature enough to resist the temptation of doing the minimum possible amount of work inherent in our system (G. Forsyth, 1966). Indeed the British system might be represented as the persistent patient versus the resistent doctor.

Quite astonishing variations also exist between countries in pharmaceutical prescribing habits both as to volume and composition (Cooper and Cooper, 1972). The *per capita* use of chloramphenicol, for example, is twenty-five times greater *per capita* in some countries than in others (Engel and Siderius, 1970). Prescriptions for vitamins are seven times more common in Britain than in say Sweden. Cholagoques and lactobacillus are both fifteen or more times greater prescribed in France than in Britain, gammaglobin, eight times more prescribed in Sweden than here and so on (Dunlop and Inch, 1972).

Probably the most important factors determining need are the patient's persistence, his ability to articulate his symptoms in a form understandable to the doctor and the resource constraints imposed upon the doctor by the supply side of the system. Collectively the medical profession appears to reassess its conception of need in line with actual levels of provision. Feldstein (1967), for example, has pointed out that any attempt to allocate funds to hospital beds based upon medical assessment of the need for them as reflected in admissions and waiting lists is likely in practice to have little or no meaning. Need grows in line with provision as doctors realign their conception of need further along the continuum. In his study of 177 large acute hospitals Feldstein found that both admissions and length of stay increased with bed availability and could discover no indication of a level of bed provision which would have fully satiated doctors' demands. Thus, like an iceberg, the more resources devoted to melting it, the more 'need' floats to the surface.

Despite an almost hundred per cent increase in the cases treated in hospital since 1949, the waiting list for admission has remained at a steady half million people which exceeds the total number of beds

TABLE 4   Waiting lists per 1,000 population and waiting times. England and Wales.

Year	Total Waiting List	Total Waiting list per thousand population	Mean Waiting Times (weeks) All causes*
1949	497,700	11.37	
1950	530,500	12.11	
1951	503,600	11.49	
1952	500,300	11.38	
1953	525,900	11.92	
1954	474,300	10.71	
1955	454,900	10.24	
1956	430,800	9.64	
1957	440,300	9.80	
1958	442,803	9.82	
1959	475,626	10.48	
1960	465,539	10.17	
1961	474,177	10.26	
1962	469,091	10.05	
1963	475,834	10.13	
1964	498,834	10.54	14.4
1965	517,142	10.84	14.5
1966	536,447	11.18	14.8
1967	537,005	11.12	14.2
1968	534,890	11.01	13.7
1969	561,365	11.50	14.0
1970	555,883	11.35	14.7
1971	525,892	10.77	13.9

* Excluding maternity in 1967-70.

Source: *Health and Personal Social Statistics for England*, HMSO 1973 and A.J. Culyer and J.G. Cullis, *New Society*, 1973.

available (Table 4). The waiting list expressed *per capita* declined slightly in the mid-fifties but is now much the same as in 1949. Over the period for which the information is available, the average waiting time has also remained static at three and a half months. The numbers of people awaiting admission has proved insensitive to increases in the services provided. Doctors appear to be assessing the need for referrals and admissions as a simple function of current provision levels. Whether or not this implies that the admissions are for increasingly trivial ailments depends, of course, upon the extent to which technological advances are increasing the range of people likely to benefit from hospitalisation. It is difficult to believe, however, that technology always outstrips provision by a constant absolute amount.

It is from a misunderstanding of the nature and imprecision of need that many of the NHS' problems have come. It is with some truth that it is said that the only fit man is one inadequately examined by his doctor. We return to this problem later but first it is necessary to examine the factors which go to determine the supply side of the health equation.

4 SUPPLY

Within the National Health Service it is the supply side of the equation which is bound to predominate. Individuals do not have to consider whether they can afford medical attention merely whether it holds out the promise of some benefit. Rational consumers will go on demanding health care until its 'marginal utility' approaches zero. Faced with almost infinite potential demand the state must decide how much of what is currently possible, scientifically and technically, it is going to make available. This simple truth, however, has been far from universally recognised. Politicians were in practice much quicker to grasp the point than the professionals who have had to work the system.

Bevan saw the NHS as a self-eliminating expense. Once the backlog of untreated sickness (pent-up demand) had been eliminated, health care expenditure would (at the very least) stabilise and possibly even decline. In practice the original bill proved to be more than double the Beveridge prediction and still showed no signs of meeting all legitimate needs. Panic ensued and urgent measures were sought to apply the brakes. In fact the growth in real expenditure was only modest and actually declined in 1953. The rapid political realisation of the insatiability of health needs, however, established patterns of spending which have persisted throughout the life of the NHS. Any expenditure capable of postponement was put to one side. Thus capital expenditure and preventive medicine were cut back in favour of current expenditure and 'crisis' medicine; caring was given second place to curing and so on. Committees were appointed to seek out forms of abuse 'and to advise how, in view of the burdens on the Exchequer a rising charge upon it [could] be avoided while providing for the maintenance of an adequate service' (Guillebaud, 1956). The pharmaceutical industries were generally attacked as profiteers in sickness and the public labelled as a nation of hypochondriacs (Cooper,

25

1966). Overwhelmed by the size of manifest demand, to this day the state has avoided as far as possible any attempt to seek out and quantify the full extent and nature of the nation's needs for health care resources. The fear persists of discovering new areas of need for which no resources exist. In 1972 the Deputy Secretary of the Department of Health and Social Security informed the Expenditure Committee that 'the fact is we are only just beginning to explore unmet need and its implication for national policy — the more we go into the problem the more we uncover, as it were, need that we have not seen before.'

Although the political lessons were learnt (perhaps too well) early on, the medical professions have only very recently begun to accept the impossibility of the early hopes for the system. Many doctors and nurses still believe that all those in need of help should get the necessary resources. They feel that their conception of adequacy is the legitimate one (even if they vary between themselves as to what it is), and that political decision makers are blind as to the real shortfall between current provision and decency. Indeed it is true that it is the practitioner who is clearly the more aware of the service the patient is receiving in practice. It is basically this conflict of viewpoint which has led to the unhappy history of professional discontent and constant prophesies of imminent doom.

The best explanation of the total allocation of expenditure in any given year between and within the social services appears to have been one based upon past levels. Basically the Treasury has allocated resources on an incremental basis. In a field like the NHS, where objectives, and criteria by which to judge their attainment, have been conspicuous by their absence, the incremental approach seemed the most obvious. It has not usually, for example, been practical politics to actually reduce any given form of expenditure.

In any labour intensive service a change in priorities can only be translated into action at best very slowly. The labour stock has not only highly specific skills but is also immobile geographically. Further, this year's capital expenditure automatically commits future current expenditure. The result is that the flexibility between different programmes open to a Minister in any one year, according to Sir William Armstrong, is unlikely to exceed 2½ per cent of the total (Select

Committee on Procedure, 1969). Any government inherits an ongoing programme from its predecessors which has an inbuilt momentum of its own. Only marginal changes are likely to be practical. Beds for geriatric patients can be expanded only as rapidly as labour can be trained or diverted from other spheres.

Klein (1974) has made the point that estimating errors, due to the difficulty of calculating the actual demands which will be made upon the social services and for social security payments a year in advance, consistently exceed conscious changes in policy. In 1973-4, for example, policy changes amounted to £1,227m as against £2,356m of estimating errors caused, amongst other factors, by the unexpected rise in unemployment benefit claims. According to Klein 'nothing could underline more forcibly the fact that changes in public expenditure reflect an accommodation to external circumstances as much as they reflect deliberate decisions.'

Since the Plowden Committee's Report (1961) there have been rigorous attempts to remove some of the undoubted former arbitrariness out of the overall allocation process. Parliament votes money annually but the Treasury now operates upon a five year rolling plan, annually surveying proposed expenditure for the next five years. These surveys are conducted by the finance officers of all the major spending departments sitting together on the Public Expenditure Survey Committee which produces a report to the Cabinet. The report projects forward the implications of present policies and lists additional programmes which could be undertaken if the resources were to be made available. This is discussed by the Cabinet, which decides the priorities and totals in the light of available resources, the end result being published as the Expenditure White Paper. The system is thus a two-way one. Information and estimates having come up from the departments, controls work back from the centre.

The general movement is towards the bringing together of financial control and policy making. Financial control formerly meant little more than ensuring that public money was spent in the authorised way by the authorised civil servants. The emphasis is now more upon why it is being spent at all. Since 1971 analytical studies of individual programmes, their objectives and any alternative methods of achieving the same ends, have been attempted under the banner of PAR (programme analysis and review). This kind of approach attempts to make explicit the positive reasons for actions and invites decision makers to scrutinise and question fully their past conventions and their present intentions.

Following the Department of Education and Science, the Department of Health and Social Security is being invited to adopt PPB (planning, programming and budgeting or, more simply, output-budgeting). This aims at a formal definition of objectives, and as a matter of regular practice looking at alternatives and monitoring progress. Once the objectives have been committed to paper, any relevant data has to be organised into appropriate programme form (for example, medical manpower and provision indices into acute, chronic, mental health programmes). Output measures have to be found to test the effectiveness of each programme and to evaluate alternative ways of achieving the same objectives. Finally, objectives and programmes need to be regularly and automatically reassessed in the light of experience and changing circumstances. All of this, of course, raises enormous issues and difficulties in practice, but it may be that in the future it will cause many traditional NHS practices to be questioned.

Expenditure

Expenditure on the NHS over the period 1953-72 rose in real terms by 130 per cent whilst total public expenditure increased by eighty-two per cent (Klein, 1974). Over this period the hospital services increased their share of current health spending from fifty-five to sixty-six per cent whilst expenditure upon the general medical services declined from twelve per cent to eight per cent (Table 5). Wages and salaries alone account for sixty-nine per cent of the current total and seventy-two per cent of the rise in expenditure since 1951.

As a percentage of national income, health expenditures have increased from 4½ per cent to 5¾ per cent (Table 6). By international standards this appears to be very modest indeed, but it is doubtful whether such comparisons mean anything. Does the higher proportion

TABLE 5 Health Services as a proportion of total cost of NHS
1950 to 1972. UK.

Year	Hospital Services	Pharma-ceutical Services	General Medical Services	General Dental Services	General Opthalmic Services	Local Health Authority Services	Other	Total
	%	%	%	%	%	%	%	%
1950	54.9	8.4	11.7	9.9	5.2	7.8	2.1	100
1951	56.0	9.8	11.0	7.8	2.8	8.4	4.2	100
1952	56.0	9.8	11.1	5.9	2.1	8.4	6.7	100
1953	55.3	9.5	10.8	5.5	2.2	8.9	7.8	100
1954	56.4	9.3	10.6	5.8	2.3	9.2	6.4	100
1955	57.3	9.6	10.2	6.3	2.5	8.7	5.4	100
1956	57.6	9.8	10.0	6.3	2.3	8.6	5.4	100
1957	57.0	9.7	10.3	6.4	2.2	8.7	5.7	100
1958	58.0	10.0	10.3	6.5	2.1	8.9	4.2	100
1959	57.4	10.1	9.7	6.5	2.1	9.3	4.9	100
1960	56.4	10.1	9.8	6.3	1.9	9.0	6.5	100
1961	56.8	9.8	9.0	6.2	1.8	9.3	7.1	100
1962	59.0	9.7	8.5	6.0	1.7	9.7	5.4	100
1963	60.1	10.1	8.3	5.7	1.6	9.9	4.3	100
1964	60.5	10.2	7.9	5.6	1.7	10.0	4.1	100
1965	60.5	11.1	7.8	5.1	1.6	10.2	3.7	100
1966	60.9	11.2	7.5	5.2	1.5	10.2	3.5	100
1967	59.9	10.6	7.9	5.0	1.4	10.7	4.5	100
1968	60.0	10.2	7.9	4.7	1.4	10.6	5.2	100
1969*	63.1	10.4	8.0	4.8	1.5	7.4	4.8	100
1970	64.2	10.0	8.3	4.9	1.4	7.0	4.4	100
1971	65.5	9.8	8.1	4.8	1.3	6.9	3.6	100
1972	66.0	9.7	7.9	4.5	1.7	6.8	3.9	100

* Change in definition of NHS. Certain local authority services transferred
from NHS to Social Services.

TABLE 6 Gross Cost of the NHS and the cost as a proportion of National Income, 1950-73 (UK)[1]

Year	Cost of NHS £ million	NHS as a % of National Income
1950	477	4.42
1951	500	4.22
1952	523	4.09
1953	548	3.98
1954	567	3.89
1955	607	3.91
1956	662	3.93
1957	721	4.04
1958	764	4.11
1959	828	4.24
1960	902	4.33
1961	981	4.40
1962	1,025	4.41
1963	1,092	4.42
1964	1,186	4.46
1965	1,308	4.62
1966	1,434	4.85
1967	1,594	5.12
1968	1,741	5.23
1969*	1,886	5.33
1970	2,083	5.38
1971	2,369	5.48
1972	2,732	5.68
1973**	3,179	5.73

1 Includes current and capital expenditure by Central and Local Government and NHS patient payments.
* Change in definition of NHS from 1969 onwards. Certain local authority services transferred from NHS to Social Services.
** 1973 is an estimate.

TABLE 7 Average annual rates of increase in expenditures for health services, consumer price index, wage index, gross national product, and population, seven countries, selected periods, 1961-9.

	Health as % GNP	Period	Health expenditures	Consumer price index	Average annual rate of increase for					Gross national product	Population
					Health expenditure adjusted for CPI changes	Wage Index	Health expenditure adjusted for wage index changes	Health expenditure adjusted by average of CPI and wage index changes			
Netherlands	5.9	1963-9	16.1	5.0	10.1	10.1	5.2	7.7		11.9	1.2
France	5.7	1963-9	14.9	3.7	10.9	7.5	7.0	9.0		10.1	0.9
Sweden	6.7	1962-9	14.0	3.9	9.2	5.3	8.2	8.7		9.8	0.7
Canada	7.3	1961-9	13.2	2.9	10.1	5.4	7.3	8.7		9.9	1.8
Federal Republic of Germany	5.7	1961-9	10.3	2.6	6.8	7.5	2.6	4.7		7.0	1.0
United States	6.8	1962-9	10.1	2.9	6.9	4.2	6.0	6.5		7.3	1.1
United Kingdom	4.8	1962-9	9.5	3.8	5.6	4.7	4.6	5.1		6.9	0.7

Source: *OHE Information Sheet* No. 22, May 1973.

of USA national income devoted to health indicate relatively more real resources or simply that the relative prices of health resources are higher in the USA and/or that the USA health care system is less efficient? In any case it is difficult to see why this argument is employed to support more health spending but not, for example, more defence! It is true, however, that health has been the poor relation of social spending in Britain. Whilst health increased its share of public spending only very modestly from 7.8 per cent in 1953 to 9.7 per cent in 1972, education increased from 6.9 per cent to 12.9 per cent and social security from 13.3 per cent to 18.9 per cent. On the capital account side, three times as much was spent on education in the 1950s and over two and a half times as much in the 1970s.

Rather more reliable than the relative shares of national income employed by health spending in different countries, is the rate of change in absolute levels of spending. Table 7 shows a fairly detailed comparison for the period 1961-9. Britain emerges bottom of the league after all adjustments except for that of a wage index deflator which has the greatest effect upon German spending.

TABLE 8 Increases in hospital revenue expenditure attributable to changes in prices and remuneration.

	Actual expenditure	Total increase	Increase due to changes in prices and remuneration	Increase in prices and remuneration as a % total increase
	£m	£m	£m	
1964-5	526	-	-	
1965-6	580	54	45	83
1966-7	637	57	42	74
1967-8	690	53	35	66
1968-9	755	65	48	74
1969-70	834	79	55	70
1970-71	983	149	121	81
1971-72	1127	144	105	73

Source: *Annual Report of the DHSS for 1970*, 1971, Cmnd 4714, p. 291.

It is clearly the hospital service which takes the bulk of NHS spending and so Tables 8 to 11 look at its expenditure in some detail. Table 8 shows that over seventy per cent of each year's rise in spending is directly attributable to increases in prices and wages. The actual increments available for additional services after this adjustment look very modest. They varied, in fact, between 1.71 per cent and 3.36 per cent of the previous years spending. In 1970-1 this would have amounted to no more than £5 per patient treated.

Table 9 shows the domination of the labour bill over hospital costing. Pharmaceuticals, for example, form only 3½ per cent of expenditure and have remained stable since the inception of the service. In terms of the average weekly cost of keeping a patient in hospital, it is nursing which emerges clearly as the forerunner.

TABLE 9   Revenue expenditure of NHS Hospitals by broad category 1949-50 and 1970-71.

	% Total 1949-50	% Total 1970-71	% Total Increase 1949/50-1970/71
Salaries and wages	58.1	69.2	72.5
Medical	(10.7)	(11.2)	(11.4)
Nursing	(22.0)	(28.0)	(29.7)
Other	(25.4)	(30.0)	(31.4)
Provisions	10.7	4.7	3.1
Uniforms and clothing	1.0	0.7	0.5
Drugs and dressings	3.4	3.5	3.4
Appliances and equipment	2.9	4.4	4.8
General services (laundry, power, etc.)	6.3	4.2	3.7
Maintenance of plant and grounds	3.4	2.6	2.5
Domestic repairs and renewals	3.4	1.2	0.7
Blood transfusion service, etc.	1.5	1.4	1.4
Central administration	2.4	3.1	3.3
Other	6.3	4.5	4.1
Total	99.4	99.5	100.0

Sources: *Annual Report of the DHSS for 1971*, 1971, Cmnd. 5019, p. 286, and *Annual Report of the Ministry of Health for 1951*, 1953, Cmnd. 8655, p. 8.

Table 10   Average Weekly Cost of maintaining an inpatient in an acute nonteaching hospital with over 100 beds in 1969-70 and 1970-71

		1969/70		1970/71	
		£	%	£	%
Inpatient wards					
1 Pay:	medical	3.10	5.4	3.98	5.8
	nursing	13.67	23.8	17.54	25.5
	domestic	2.77	4.8	3.09	4.5
	other	0.39	0.7	0.45	0.7
2 Drugs		1.62	2.8	1.83	2.7
3 Dressings:	prepacked	0.47	0.8	0.18	0.3
	other			0.37	0.5
4 Patients' appliances		0.05	0.1	0.06	0.1
5 Equipment:	major	0.09	0.2	0.12	0.2
	other – traditional	1.27	2.2	0.99	1.4
	disposable			0.50	0.1
6 Contract services		0.08	0.1	0.09	0.1
7 Ward Total		(23.51)	(40.92)	(29.20)	(42.51)
Other treatment departments					
1 Operating theatres		5.70	9.9	7.03	10.2
2 Radiography		0.14	0.2	0.19	0.3
3 Diagnostic X-rays		1.01	1.8	1.15	1.7
4 Pathology		1.93	3.4	2.34	3.4
5 Physiotherapy		0.36	0.6	0.46	0.7
6 Pharmacy		0.50	0.9	0.60	0.9
7 Ancillary medical service		0.51	0.9	0.66	1.0
8 Total		(10.15)	(17.66)	(12.43)	(18.09)
Nontreatment departments					
1 Nurses in training		0.81	1.4	1.05	1.5
2 Catering		6.07	10.6	6.46	9.4
3 Staff residences		2.15	3.7	2.30	3.3
4 Laundry		1.20	2.1	1.28	1.9
5 Power, light and heat		1.88	3.3	2.01	2.9
6 Building maintenance		1.93	3.4	2.62	3.8
7 Medical records		0.50	0.9	0.59	0.9
8 General administration		2.54	4.4	2.92	4.3
9 General portering		1.38	2.3	1.59	2.3
10 General cleaning		0.55	1.0	0.65	0.9
11 Maintenance of grounds		0.23	0.4	0.26	0.4
12 Transport		0.23	0.4	0.28	0.4
13 Other		4.35	7.6	5.04	7.3
14 Total		(23.79)	(41.40)	(27.05)	(39.38)
	TOTAL	57.45		68.68	

Source: *Annual Reports of the DHSS*, 1970 and 1971.

Nursing forms twenty-eight per cent of total costs and it is rising. Also worthy of note is the fact that the nontreatment departments account for no less than forty per cent of total costs. Doctors, however, account for only £3.98 per week (or 5.8 per cent). This statistic above all others indicates the economy of collective provision. It is difficult to imagine any private system in which the patient's bill for medical supervision came to such a modest weekly amount! Medical expenditure is less than the combined costs of portering and maintenance (Table 10).

Table 11 divides expenditure up amongst the broad medical departments showing the relatively poor share of the psychiatric and geriatric departments despite their accounting for forty-two per cent of the beds. We return to this later.

TABLE 11 Estimated breakdown of hospital expenditure into broad departments. England and Wales 1970-71.

	Inpatient Expenditure £ million	Outpatient Expenditure £ million	Total £ million	%
Medical Departments	156.1	38.6	194.7	20.9
Surgical Departments	217.2	66.1	283.3	30.5
Geriatrics/Chronic Sick	91.0	0.5	91.5	9.8
Psychiatric a) Mental Illness	131.3	7.6	138.9	14.8
b) Mental Handicap	61.9	(0.04)	61.9	6.7
Obstetrics/GP Maternity	50.0	10.3	60.3	6.5
Accident & Emergency		51.1	51.1	5.5
Other	44.9	2.1	47.0	5.1
Total	752.3	176.4	928.7	100.0

Source: (For totals) Supply Estimates 1971-2; (for breakdown) *DHSS Annual Report 1971* and *Hospital Costing Returns*, OHE Information Sheets.

Provision of Services

After a slight increase in the early years the number of beds provided
has declined from 453,000 to 450,000 and from 10.3 to 9.2 per
thousand population. All the indicators of hospital work load however
have increased considerably. The number of inpatients treated, for
example, has doubled to some six million. Patients treated per bed
has doubled as a consequence from 6.6 to 12.3. New outpatients also
increased by seventy-three per cent from 1949 to 1971. There are
no completely reliable indicators of how general practice work loads
have changed, but what evidence there is suggests that consultation
rates have probably remained fairly steady around three and a half
per patient per year but that home visits as a percentage of all consultations have declined by some sixty per cent (Royal College of General
Practitioners, 1973).

This massive increase in work load and through-put per head has
been accompanied by very large increases in medical and other manpower. Table 12 shows that the numbers of hospital doctors, nurses
and administrative staff all increased one hundred per cent and technical and professional workers increased in number 150 per cent. At
the same time all the executive council services increased by fifteen
per cent or less. All this can be set against the increase in the population
of only eleven per cent. Over the period 1966-70, for example, manpower increased at rates in excess of all work load indicators. Dis-
charges and deaths increased 8½ per cent, new outpatients five per
cent, accident and emergency patients 4½ per cent, but doctors 15½
per cent, nurses nine per cent and professional and technical staff
twenty per cent.

Despite these large increases in manpower — trends which imply
that by the early twenty-first century half the population will be employed in hospitals — there have been continuous complaints of
shortage. In June of this year (1974) the Hospital Consultants and
Specialists Association claimed, upon the basis of a postal survey of
their members, that even current work loads demanded a doubling
of their numbers (Da Costa, 1974). They did not tell us, however,

TABLE 12 Manpower Changes 1949-71 (England and Wales).

	Unit	1949	1971	% change
Hospital Service				
Ancillary staff (porters, etc.)	No	157,112	239,770	52.6
Professional and technical	Wte	13,940	36,817	164.1
Medical staff	Wte	11,735	23,806	102.9
(consultants)		(3,488)	(8,655)	(148.1)
Dental staff	Wte	206	753	265.5
Nursing staff	No	137,636	288,065	109.3
Administrative and clerical	No	23,797	47,690	100.4
Regional Board staff	No	1,320	7,243	448.7
Executive Council				
General practitioners (all principals)	No	20,400	23,707	16.2
Dentists	No	9,495	10,962	15.5
Opthalmic medical practitioners	No	996	920	-7.6
Population	(000)	43,785	48,815	11.5

Source: Various Reports of the Ministry and Department of Health 1950-72. Wte — whole time equivalents.

whether this implied that only half the work currently considered necessary was in fact being carried out or whether they simply felt that they should be called upon to work only half as hard (a not uncommon feeling). Nor did they raise the question as to whether only half as many patients should be treated at all. Further, throughout 1974 the nurses' representatives have been claiming shortfalls in their numbers amounting to crisis dimensions. What has not been accepted generally by the medical and allied professions is that conditions of shortage are normal and unavoidable in any system or avenue of human endeavour. Resources being limited and needs infinite, shortage is with us for ever. The question is whether the degree of shortage in the NHS is relatively less acceptable to society than the degrees of shortage experienced in other walks of life. Viewed in this light it is difficult to substantiate the claim that, in the case of manpower at least, the NHS has been relatively deprived. Indeed the massive expansion in numbers within the hospital system rather suggests that sometimes labour has been used almost as if it were a free good. Problems have been tackled by sending yet another wave of troops over the trench walls. The question is what are the troops achieving towards winning the war once in the thick of battle?

The NHS has found it easier to ask for more than to examine and question critically its current deployment of resources. There is, of course, only a limited pool of manpower to draw upon and the NHS must share this pool with other legitimate claimants. Between them health and education claim thirty-seven per cent of all degree level workers. In something of an understatement, J.M. Last (1969) remarked that 'often social institutions besides medicine have a claim on the available pool of talent from which doctors are recruited. It is possible that medicine already receives its fair share.' The same, of course, applies to nurses. Nurse recruitment is heavily dependent upon the eighteen-year old age group of which it already claims approximately seven per cent.

Evidence of shortfalls from generally accepted standards of adequacy clearly do exist, however, *within* the NHS. Despite increases in the labour force, in long stay wards there remains evidence of overwork by anybody's standards. The geriatric, chronic, long stay and psychiatric hospitals and some special units, simply do not get their share of resources. Further, there are severe regional and hospital inequalities (see the section on planning and management) and shortages of certain grades of labour (e.g. staff nurses). Putting these right is not, however, simply a question of more funds for the NHS. It is a question of NHS priorities in its deployment of scarce labour resources. The early obstacle to the expansion of renal dialysis units was not so much the cash but rather the shortage of technical staff to man them (Robinson, 1966).

Despite the large and growing number of nurses at any one time, only fifty per cent are qualified, twenty-five per cent are in training and twenty-five per cent are auxiliaries. Only £134 per year is spent on giving a nurse her skills, compared with £1,300 spent upon undergraduates. Wastage is high and vocal dissatisfaction with working conditions and pay persistent. Disenchantment appears universal. Even at Guy's Hospital where some 3,000 girls apply for only 200 vacancies, turnover is rapid. Technical staff are equally difficult to retain once trained. Radiographers leave Guy's on average after only eighteen months and physiotherapists after thirty months. Nationally, thirty per cent of all student nurses leave without finishing their training. Over fifteen per cent of all nurses and twenty-six per cent of all new entrants were born overseas (Green, 1974).

Last year a record number of doctors were added to the register. Nevertheless it is still relatively easy to argue the case for more. Over thirty per cent of all hospital doctors were born overseas. Similarly fifteen per cent of all general practitioners. Britain currently imports at least four hundred long stay doctors a year from countries like India and Nigeria, with doctor-patient ratios of 0.17 and 0.02 per 1,000 respectively whilst exporting simultaneously four hundred British-born doctors to the USA and Canada with ratios of 1.60 as against our own of 1.2 (Gish, 1971). Our export of doctors to Canada is particularly unfortunate. Marc Lalonde, the Canadian Minister of Health, recently urged tight controls upon the import of foreign-born doctors into Canada as they already have 'too many'! Nearly one half of their annual addition of doctors are immigrants, the UK providing about thirty per cent of these (Lalonde, 1974). Doctors have very high international mobility and many wish to sell their skills for the highest price. All professional skills tend to attract higher remuneration in the USA, Canada, France and Germany than in the UK, but few have the same opportunities to take advantage of the fact. Nearer to home, sensitivity to pay rates has recently been illustrated in the Republic of Ireland which has found itself with a surplus of junior hospital doctors as a result of a pay award which left their pay scales higher than those in the UK.

Again, certain 'unfashionable' areas of medicine have impossibly large ratios of nursing, medical and ancillary staff. Expenditure per patient week on the mentally ill for nursing is only forty-six per cent of that in acute hospitals, on doctors, twenty-six per cent and on total inpatient costs, thirty-four per cent. Further, eighty-three per cent of all registrars and sixty-five per cent of all senior registrars in, for example, geriatrics were born overseas, as were seventy-five per cent of all junior doctors for all specialities in the Newcastle Regional Board area. Conditions have been described in which one consultant tends to 660 mentally ill patients (indeed the average in 1971 was one to 154) and in which wards have over fifty beds, many with less than two feet between them. Robb (1967) described degrading and disgraceful practices and conditions which went on too long without attention for comfort. Even in 1972 the Director of the Hospital Advisory Service was able to say that 'it is possible to find wards in mental hospitals where patients sleep, eat, excrete, live and die in one large room.' Set up in 1969, the function of the Advisory Service is not to uncover scandals but to provide, as visitors to long term institutions, a means of alerting Ministers to situations in which scandalous conditions and practices could arise if left unchecked and unaided (Brown, 1973).

Buildings

Capital account spending is in the short run the easiest to postpone but in the long run builds up problems of overwhelming proportions. Over the first thirteen years of the NHS only one new hospital opened its doors. Indeed proportionally less was spent on building than in the 1930s. The Powell plan for hospital building envisaged 90 new and 134 substantially remodelled hospitals by 1972 — in practice the figure was forty (HMSO, 1962).

The NHS inherited an obsolete capital stock. About thirty per cent were former Local Government institutions, often sited away from population concentrations (e.g. mental and isolation hospitals) or built 'for' the sick poor. The rest of the stock consisted of the old voluntary hospitals which ranged from the great London teaching hospitals to small and randomly located 'philanthropic accidents.' As a consequence fifty per cent of our bed stock is in buildings built before 1900 and offering facilities in many respects more akin to a railway station than a place for the ailing. Only about eighteen per cent of the beds are in new or replacement buildings provided under the NHS.

Despite this somewhat gloomy story, capital expenditure as a percentage of total current expenditure has been rising rapidly. Under four per cent in the early 1950s, it now exceeds twelve per cent, and is eleven per cent of the total NHS budget. Had capital been more readily forthcoming in the 1950s undoubtedly the hospital stock would have been over expanded by contemporary standards. Whereas opinion in the early days of the NHS was that the system needed fifty per cent more beds, by the time of the Powell Plan in 1962 a reduction in the bed to population ratio was being urged. Professional conservatism had become adjusted to shortened lengths of stay and increased through-puts (Brown, 1973). Long term plans are now for three hundred new district hospitals (of which 190 are complete or under construction) with yet lower ratios and at great economy, for a saving of one bed per thousand population represents a cut of over £1m. a year in running costs and £3m. in capital costs for a district hospital serving a population catchment area of a quarter of a million.

Although in 1969 the Bonham-Carter Report considered that it would be uneconomic to provide specialist care outside of the district general hospitals and indeed suggested that patients who did not require the high level of service offered in the district hospital should not be in hospital at all, a government statement of August 1974 saw a role for 'community hospitals.' Basically these are seen as providing minor surgery, accident work and hospital beds for those who need to be hospitalised as they cannot be properly cared for at home. General practitioners would have responsibility for day to day care. In practice this is likely to mean a reprieve for existing small hospitals rather than the building of new ones.

Adequacy and the Supply of Doctors

In 'normal' price markets, shortage is signalled by rising prices which attract additional resources into that area of production. In the absence of any such automatic signal, shortage can only mean a short-fall from some technically determined standard of adequacy. Unfortunately there is no simple or universally acceptable method of determining adequacy in this sense. Technical experts have an interest in always demanding more and will tend to adjust their concept of adequacy through time in line with whatever current provision levels happen to be. Often they appear to be saying little more than that it is better to have more rather than less of a desirable commodity or service. The so-called 'shortage' of doctors is, as we have seen, a case in point.

As it takes six years to train a doctor, adequacy is dependent upon the somewhat hazardous task of projecting the Service's manpower needs half a decade or so in advance. Many of the projections since the inception of the NHS have probably resulted in rather more harm than good on balance. Henry Willink's Committee set up in 1955 has been universally condemned for recommending a ten per cent cutback in the medical schools' intake and yet there is little evidence that the lessons of this 'mistake' have been fully understood. There were clearly a number of factors contributing to Willink's decision. First, his projection was based upon a population increase of only 4.5 per cent between 1955-71, while, in the event, population increased over eight per cent. This population forecast was a datum for Willink and little purpose is served by criticism on this score. Second, the Committee paid scant regard to the possibility of emigration. It considered that there was 'no doubt that the opportunities for doctors from Great Britain to obtain employment overseas have been diminishing in the recent past and will continue to do so in the future,' though at the same time it acknowledged the inadequacy of the available data (HMSO, 1957). Subsequently, it was shown that in the latter half of the 1950s nearly a quarter of the British-born medical school graduates were emigrating, the loss being felt mainly by the hospital service (J.R. Seale, 1962; B. Abel-Smith, 1964). Much the most important source of error lay in their implicit assumption that the then prevalent ratio of doctors to population would be deemed adequate by the experts of 1971.

There are now twice as many doctors *per capita* as there were in the 1920s, but of course there have also been (largely unknown) changes in work load caused by the changing structure and medical progress (OHE, 1966). Since the inception of the NHS, with the exceptions of 1959 and 1963, doctors have consistently increased more rapidly than population. In the early years there were about 710 doctors (hospital plus general practitioners) per million population. This rose to 840 by 1959, was 892 in 1969 and 937 by 1971. At the time Willink reported both hospital and general practice doctors were rising steadily in numbers and concern was being expressed in some quarters of the profession as to future monetary and career prospects. The *Lancet* (1957, p. 1043) was prompted to warn that 'an excess of doctors would be a bad thing,' whilst the *BMJ* (1957, 1. 1,227) commented that the report was the outcome of 'a growing feeling by many, including the Representative Body of the BMA and the Conference of Local Medical Committees, that perhaps too many doctors were being trained for too few openings in the future and that a surplus during the next few years was inevitable.' After the Willink recommendations (although not necessarily as a result of them) the number of general practitioners fell slightly and has remained fairly static ever since.

The Royal Commission on Medical Education (1968), alarmed at the lack of growth in general practitioner numbers, and the exodus of hospital doctors to more lucrative employment overseas, recommended a fifty per cent increase in the output of our medical schools over the next twenty-five years. The Commission (which was composed of ten doctors and six laymen) pointed out that there was 'no absolute or optimum level of health services which can be measured and towards which we can aim.' Their estimation of future requirements was, in the event, based upon doctor ratios in other countries (they have, for example, almost half as many people per doctor in the USSR and eighty per cent as many in the USA as in the UK), the effects of an ageing population and so on. Little account, if any, was taken of the scope for the substitution of capital for labour, or of one kind of skill for another or of the scope for economies in the current deployment of labour. Certainly the basic problem in determining adequacy has been the absence of a clearly defined objective. How much more difficult then, for the Royal Commission to anticipate such a definition for the future.

Whether we have sufficient doctors depends upon a listing of overall priorities for skilled manpower throughout the economy. It cannot be judged in isolation and in any case there is no technically obvious level of provision. Shortage is, of course, normal. How many doctors there are is a decision reflecting society's current priorities within the overall constraints imposed by total resources. Clearly such decisions will be less arbitrary if we have a clear picture of the tasks we wish doctors to perform. For example both preventive medicine with yearly check-ups and a planned expansion of the use of medical auxiliaries with growing emphasis upon community care would profoundly influence the desired doctor-population ratio. To date society has given no clear lead as to what it expects of its doctors, whilst they, themselves, have revealed widely differing conceptions of their true roles. Wide variations in all aspects of their workloads have been reported between practices of comparable size and age composition (Lees and Cooper, 1963). Richardson (1973), for example, has reported a more than threefold variation in consultation rate per patient in his study of 143 practices in northern Scotland. To the extent that consultations are doctor determined, this suggests that some doctors view their role as at least in part to lend an ear to the problems of the lonely or to those with acute personal problems, whilst others discourage all but the strictly medical. This may go far towards explaining why John Fry (1972) can report the experiences of an excellently managed practice coping with 4,500 patients (more than twice the national average) without any obvious signs of strain whilst at the same time practice lists of only 2,000 are being actively urged as the technical assessment of adequacy. Clearly current numbers of general practitioners are perfectly consistent with maintaining that there exists either a surplus or deficit according to the view taken as to a doctor's proper pastoral and medical role (OHE, 1974).

In any event the policy of hoping that an expansion in overall numbers will eventually rectify the regional and other irregularities within the NHS must be finally abandoned and a determined policy of rational deployment of any additional manpower by financial and other inducements be embarked upon. Society cannot afford for example to 'over expand' its supply of neuro-surgeons in the hope that, as a byproduct, it will increase its supply of child psychiatrists to more acceptable levels.

5 THE NEED TO RATION

No country is as healthy as it could be and certainly no country can afford to do as much for the sick as is currently technically feasible. Avoidable death is part of everyday experience. Nor can it be said that health is necessarily the most important of competing goals. Daily people eat too much, drink to excess, smoke and take unnecessary risks. Given the inexactness of need and the almost unlimited scope for the individual to consider himself unwell, clearly it is impossible for any society to eliminate all need. Available resources must somehow be rationed among competing claims. In the health service this problem has fallen to the medical and allied professions. Clearly want, demand and need are interrelated with actual provision, whilst in turn, actual provision will to some extent reflect medical assessment of need. Need will depend upon not only medical progress and the patients' demands but also upon factors largely personal to the individual doctor.

Figure 1 illustrates the process of matching demand to supply. The general practitioner is the initial gate keeper of the system. It is he who controls whether a demand stops at a visit to his surgery or goes on to combine time, pharmaceuticals and hospital resources. Table 13 illustrates the possibilities.

Before proceeding to discuss the rationing process in practice it is useful to attempt to illustrate the economic implications of the NHS graphically. Figure 2 is the conventional supply and demand curve diagram so beloved of first year economics students.

In the 'normal' market the demand for goods and services is equated with available supply by movements in price. In the health market the price is in effect zero. Rational economic behaviour dictates that an individual faced with a zero price (free) commodity or service will consume it until further consumption yields him or her no further utility — that is until he has no further use for it. In the case of health

FIGURE 1   The accommodation of want to supply

WANT	DEMAND	NEED
An individual's own assessment of his health state. His 'want' for better health	Those of his wants that the individual converts into demand by seeking the assistance of a medical practitioner	A state of health assessed as in need of treatment by a medical practitioner. Not all demands will become needs and not all needs will find expression as demands

RELATIVE NEED		WAITING LISTS	
Total Health resources must be distributed amongst competing needs by the medical assessment of relative degrees of need	**+**	Those needs currently recognised by the medical profession but for which there are currently no resources	**=**

HEALTH CARE RESOURCES	TOTAL PUBLIC EXPENDITURE	NATION'S TAX POTENTIAL
Share of current spending reflects current government priorities and their assessment of the relative cases put by the various spending authorities	Reflects not only taxation raised but also current general economic policy	Theoretical limit to society's willingness to substitute public goods, services and transfer payments for direct command over private goods and services

47

TABLE 13

The NHS Rationing Process

Patient's Own Assessment	Action Taken	GP's Assessment	Action Taken	Specialist's Assessment	Medical Action Taken	Effect
1) In Want	1) Sees Doctor	1) In Need	1) Refers	1) In Need	1) Treatment a) Proven b) Unproven c) Unsound d) Inappropriate e) Alleviate f) Comforting 2) No Treatment a) None technically possible b) None available c) Low priority 3) Second Best Treatment	1) No effect 2) Cure 3) Survival 4) Death 5) Reassurance
				2) Not In Need	1) Referred Back 2) Self Medication	As above
			2) Treated	None	1) As with Specialist	As above
				None	1) Second Opinion 2) Self Medication	As above
		2) Not In Need	None	None	1) Self Medication 2) Advised to see doctor	As above
	2) Sees Pharmacist	None	None	None	None	1) Survival 2) Death
	3) None	None	None	None	None	As above
2) Not in Want	None	None	None	None	None	As above

Source: Taken from M.H. Cooper, 'Rationing and Financing Health Care Resources' in N. Hunt and W.D. Reekie (eds), *Management and the Social Services*, Tavistock Press, 1974.

FIGURE 2 The Supply and Demand for Health Resources

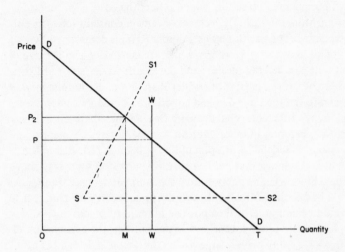

Explanatory Key: DD is a market demand line for health resources.
This shows the quantity of resources that would be demanded at various prices.

SS1 and SS2 are two possible supply lines each indicating the quantity of resources that would be supplied by resource owners at various prices.

WW is the actual level of public provision. As this is administratively determined it will not vary with changes in prices and hence can be represented by a vertical line.

P is the market clearing price given that OW is being supplied.

this is likely to approach infinity or at any rate so high a level of consumption that it may as well be infinity. In Figure 2 demand at zero price is shown as a large but finite quantity of health resources OT.

In a normal market, supply would reflect the costs of production. These might increase (SS1), decrease or remain constant (SS2) as output expanded. The health service's supply (OW) is determined by a series of administrative decisions, which are constrained by the size of the current national tax receipts and the health service's share of them. Whether OW proved greater or smaller than that under normal market provision (given the same demand conditions) would depend upon the actual shape of the cost related supply line. SS1 would result in less, whilst SS2, in more. In theory at least the health service's share of total resources is dependent upon public opinion as reflected in the ballot box. Assuming that public provision must stop some way short of utopia there will inevitably follow some unmet demand. In practice this will be less than WT, as although the price is zero, the true cost to the would be consumer will be positive in terms of inconvenience, bus fares, lost leisure or work time and so on. Further, the expectation of resource availability plays a large part in determining demand at a fixed price. Demand tends to gravitate in the long run towards whatever level of provision OW happens to be. Few will queue for resources they know not to exist.

In the normal market if the supply were OW then it would be rationed amongst potential demanders according to their willingness and ability to pay a price equal to P. In practice the supply would be determined by actual supply costs. If, for example, SS1 were the supply line then OM would be supplied and demanded at price P2. Those unable to pay P2 due to limited financial resources and/or other claims on their spending power would simply have to go without. In the NHS rationing must take place in some other manner.

The NHS attempts to ration the scarce resources allocated to it by governments, not in accordance with the individual's ability and willingness to pay, but in accordance with each individual's relative need. 'Need' is a physical or mental state considered to require attention by an acknowledged expert or experts — for the most part a medical practitioner.

Individuals express not 'need' but 'demand,' demand being in turn 'expressed want.' A person's 'want' is his own self-assessment of his health state. If he chooses to take some action as a consequence of his assessment, then he expresses his want in the form of 'demand.' It is at this point that the health service omits a stage from the normal market process. The individual does not have to consider whether, in view of competing claims for his financial resources, he can 'afford' to take action. That is, demand is not narrowed into 'effective demand' (want or desire backed up by both the ability and willingness to pay). Further, as the NHS does not have to 'price' its services, there is no automatic indication of the position and shape of its 'cost' lines.

The NHS attempts to narrow down 'expressed wants' (demands) to match available resources by means of doctors' technical assessments of patients' relative needs. As we have seen, however, need is not an absolute state but a matter of judgment and opinion. It is one of many possible points along one of many possible continuums. Each doctor is liable to have his own dividing line between states that are categorised as being in need and those free of need.

FIGURE 3   Need and the Waiting List

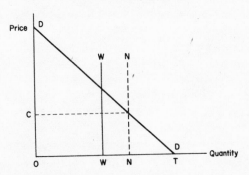

Explanatory Key: DD & WW as in Figure 2.
C is the effective value of all deterrents to patients converting wants into demands (NT).
WN is the waiting list.

51

In Figure 3 need (ON) is shown to lie somewhere to the right of OW (actual provision) and to the left of OT (demand). In practice NT fails to manifest itself due to a range of implicit and explicit deterrents (rationing devices) including travel, time, convenience, receptionist's attitudes and so on. The gap WN, however, represents current waiting lists. WN is the excess need recognised and acted upon by general practitioners. Clearly this will reflect current provision levels. Should OW grow, then doctors will refer more patients and maintain the gap-WN. Haywood (1974) cites some actual examples of this happening in his experience as an administrator.

Although the medical and allied professions have never seen their function as anything other than aiding the sick they are nonetheless implicitly or explicitly daily involved in rationing decisions. Finance and manpower can never come near to the full potential of need or demand. The welfare of the patient, the interests of the professions and the economy of the public purse are complexly interrelated. The next section looks at rationing at work.

6 RATIONING IN PRACTICE

It is of course questionable whether doctors see their role as 'rationing' at all. They insist upon the complete 'clinical freedom' to treat each and every patient in the manner which they individually see to be in their best interests and without any *ex post* accountability. They are 'accountable only to the patients whom they serve and to their own conscience' (Cook, 1972).

Medicine has a long tradition of being heroic and individualistic. The belief in clinical freedom is deep seated. Given that need was absolute and that the nation could afford to allocate whatever level of resources proved necessary to meet it, then granting the profession immunity from normal market forces would be possible and probably desirable. Clearly, however, this is not the case. In most professions freedom to do whatever is best for the client is constrained by his ability to pay: in the medical profession it is constrained by the state's ability to pay. The general practitioner decides whether resources are used up or whether the patient returns home empty handed and, hopefully, reassured. In practice some ninety per cent of all episodes of illness are dealt with from start to finish by the general practitioner (Ashford and Pearson, 1970). General practitioners, however, display no consistency in the number of episodes of sickness which they deem as worthy of a referral to a consultant (Scott and Gilmore, 1966), the number and type of prescriptions they write (Weatherall, 1964), the number of home visits they make or in any other quantifiable aspect of their work (Lees and Cooper, 1963). More than twofold variations in work load between practices with similar lists and catchment areas can only be explained by reference to how the doctor himself conceives his job.(Royal College of General Practitioners, 1968). As independent contractors, general practitioners clearly have a wide range of discretion and use it.

There is growing evidence that appointment systems (now used by some sixty per cent of practices in contrast to six per cent in 1961) act as barriers rather than as aids to patient contacts (OHE, 1974). W.O. Williams (1970) has shown, for example, that the consultation rate for practices operating a full appointments system is lower than for those without one. People who wake up with a pain are not usually interested in seeing their doctor in three days time. Further, it is often adding insult to injury to have to wait for a further two hours after waiting three days and arriving on time. More and more patients appear to be bypassing their general practitioner and presenting themselves to their local casualty department where eventually they get service. The Chief Medical Officer of Health (1972) has pointed to the increased use of the appointment system as at least a partial explanation of the fifty per cent increase in new patients attending accident and emergency departments between 1959 and 1970. Further, a study of casualty departments revealed that at least seventy per cent of its work load was well within the competence of a nurse or general practitioner and should not have been presented to the hospital to deal with (Nuffield Provincial Hospitals Trust, 1960). Of course, failure to get an early appointment is not the only possible explanation for this trend. A man waking up in the morning may be undecided as to whether his pain is sufficiently acute to merit a visit to his doctor. By the time he has travelled to work, however, the pain may have become worse and all doubt left him (HMSO, 1974a).

On the question of referrals to specialists, J.M. Last found that amongst ninety-four doctors, three referred less than five persons per thousand seen whilst at the other extreme, one referred 115 (Last, 1967). Scott and Gilmore (1966) found a variation in the proportion of patients referred to hospital during a year, between practices in Edinburgh, of from 0.6 per cent to 25.8 per cent whilst Forsyth and Logan (1968) could find no explanation for such variations, although commenting upon the variation in quality and detail of the referral letters. Although as many as eighty-three per cent of referrals to consultant surgeons have been found to go no further than an initial interview without any pathological or X-ray investigation (Forsyth and Logan, 1968), Ashford and Pearson have shown that, in Exeter at least, those general practitioners with high referral rates also have

54

high hospital admission rates (Ashford and Pearson, 1970). Studies have also shown admission rates to vary between doctors in Barrow from 41.3 to 107.9 per thousand patients (Forsyth and Logan, 1960), whilst consultants' waiting list decisions have been shown to be equally variable. In a study of ninety-two hospitals, forty-six reported that the person who authorised the placing of a name on the waiting list was the consultant concerned whilst thirty nine stated it was either the consultant, SHMO or the registrar. When asked whether there were any accepted medical criteria for inclusion on the waiting list, forty-one replied in the negative. In stating that there was no accepted criterion for inclusion on the list, one hospital said:

'inclusion on the list is based on the assessment of the medical condition of the patient by the individual consultant in charge of the case. The medical criteria therefore vary according to the individual standards of each consultant although there would certainly be a *level* at which all consultants would agree, that a case should be included on the waiting list.'
(Institute of Hospital Administrators 1963)

The Scott and Gilmore study (1966) pointed out that of those patients attending outpatients departments three or more times, fifty per cent had been referred by the general practitioner for 'an opinion only'!

Once admitted to hospital both the legitimacy of many new patients being there and their length of stay are being challenged increasingly and wide variations in practice revealed. Studies have found that as many as forty per cent of all acute patients need not have been hospitalised on medical grounds (Butler, 1970). Crombie and Cross (1959), for example, found that twenty-five per cent of the patients in the male medical wards of a Birmingham hospital had no therapeutic or diagnostic need to be there. For females the rate was forty-two per cent. The length of stay for any given condition varies many fold between hospitals, even after standardisation for age and sex, and rejecting extreme values which show high fluctuations from year to year. The variations between length of stay following treatment of hernia is fivefold, for appendicitis is sixfold, and for bronchitis and pneumonia ninefold. Heasman (1964) found that the removal of adenoids and tonsils from children over fifteen years old resulted in a six day stay for over eighty per cent of all cases in one hospital group but in a stay of only one day in over fifty per cent of the cases of another. Heasman and Carstairs (1971) found that the median duration of stay between consultants treating at least twenty peptic ulcers during one year ranged from six to twenty-six days, whilst that between physicians treating myocardial infarction from ten to thirty-six days. The overall variation in average length of stay for all conditions between the regions is currently fifty-three per cent. Clearly if all hospitals and regions adopted the practices of the higher extremes the cost implications for the NHS would be enormous. Maxwell (1974) has put the length of stay issue into stark relief with the observation that if France were to adopt the USA standard of twenty-seven cases per bed per year, it could manage its current work load with only fifty-five per cent of its current hospital capacity.

Little or no evidence exists to support the contention that those doctors and consultants who habitually insist upon using more resources are in reality materially altering the medical condition of their patients. In the case of hernia, for example, Morris et al (1968) established that discharge from hospital after one day had no observable effect upon the patient compared with discharge after one week. The current national average stay for this condition, however, remains eleven days whilst some hospitals average twenty-one days.

Clearly different doctors are taking different actions when confronted with similar health states. This is not, of course, to argue that either human beings or their ailments are all exactly similar. Clearly patients cannot all be discharged after the minimum length of stay irrespective of their actual medical condition. What could be suggested, however, is that patients should be discharged after the minimum acceptable period in the clear absence of any good reason to the contrary. There should always be explicit and positive reasons for variations from the scientifically established practice.

Whilst it is true that doctors have to adjust their aggregate demands so that they are consistent with available resources, clinical freedom means that they are individually neither adjusting from, nor to, a common base line or conception of need. What one general practitioner sees as meriting a referral will still differ radically from that of another even if all general practitioners are forced to adjust to changed supply circumstances.

Clinical freedom is, of course, also the freedom to be wrong. There is a growing body of evidence that much medical practice is, if not unsound, then at least unproven (Cochrane, 1972). Large scale cancer surgery, insulin treatment for diabetes, tonsillectomy and hospital bed rest for both coronary heart disease and TB are some examples which have been examined and found wanting.

Surgery for small cell cancer of the bronchus has, for example, been shown by controlled trials to lessen, rather than lengthen, a patient's life expectancy compared with treatment by radiotherapy alone (MRC, 1966). Again, in the case of TB, the World Health Organisation has shown that even in the poorest areas of Madras treatment at home was no less effective than that in hospital (Laing, 1971). Yet in Britain the average length of stay in hospital remains at seventy days. Further, in a survey of six hospitals twenty per cent of male patients with pulmonary tuberculosis in one hospital had a stay of over 360 days, but all were discharged in under ninety days in another. In three hospitals admitting comparable cases, ten per cent, fifty-two per cent and eighty-two per cent respectively of patients had had at least one tomogram (Cochrane, 1972).

H. Mather and his colleagues (1971) found by means of a randomised controlled trial in Bristol that hospital treatment (including a variable time in a coronary care unit) showed no positive medical gain over treatment at home for acute ischaemic heart disease. Indeed sheer fright at being placed in a coronary unit may well have contributed to cardiac arrests.

Perhaps even more serious is the literature pointing to the rise of iatrogenic disease or DOMP (diseases of medical practice). Malleson (1973) quotes the story of Harry Solomon at Harvard who added to his medical reputation by curing patients over fifty years old of being confused and forgetful by denying them their usual supply of prescribed barbiturates. A dramatic example of global DOMP was revealed by a study conducted in Hanover, which suggested that the main reason for the German mortality rate from appendicitis being three times higher than any other country was that appendectomy was performed there three times as often. A follow up of 959 cases revealed that only one in four patients had actually been suffering from acute appendicitis. The appendix was healthy but the patient dead (Lichtner and Pflanz, 1971). In the USA a decline in the appendectomy rate has been accompanied by a parallel fall in the mortality rate.

It is certain that much medical treatment is inappropriate, unproven or even unsound but will authorities ever be united in deciding which? Indeed, even if there were unanimity as to which treatments did no positive good does it follow that they would be universally discontinued as unnecessary? Such treatment, it could be claimed, provides hope and temporary reassurance to many otherwise hopeless cases. Few doctors are prepared to tell a patient that the hope of effective treatment is so low that he should go home and wait unaided to recover or die. The question is, however, what level of resources can the country afford to allocate to such ends however desirable and, again, having decided this, ought there not to be some uniformity of practice between doctors and hospitals?

Very little current medical practice has ever been subjected to the same rigorous testing to which, say, all new pharmaceuticals are subjected. The objection to evaluation of medical and surgical practices seems to centre upon the ethics of denying a control group of patients a possibly helpful treatment, purely as a consequence of a random numbers table. There seems, however, to be little justification in this objection in those cases where the treatment is already widely considered suspect. Bed rest, for example, appears to be an admirable candidate for evaluation. It is expensive in resources and practice already varies widely throughout the country.

Considerable work is now under way in some of these areas. Research, for example, into the optimal period of stay following elective surgery for hernia and varicose veins has been reported (Matthew, 1971). In Scotland, information is being sent confidentially to each consultant about how his practices compare with those of his colleagues. This gives the opportunity at least of rational adjustment and/or of controlled trials in cooperation with colleagues. There is, however, little point in evaluation if clinical freedom is to continue to mean freedom to be eccentric and ignore scientific evidence without any attempts to refute it. Certainly Dollery's (1971) suggestion of an independent audit group with the authority to visit and investigate has fallen upon largely stony ground. It did represent a means of professional advice and guidance being given by colleagues to and from colleagues. In fact the lack of reaction to his paper rather suggests that the profession felt unable to take it at all seriously (Forsyth, 1973).

The whole rationale of clinical freedom may be increasingly questioned. Rationing in the NHS has never been explicitly organised but has hidden behind each doctor's clinical freedom to act solely in the interests of his individual patient. Any conflict of interest between patients competing for scarce resources has been implicitly resolved by the doctors' judgments as to their relative needs for care and attention. The clinical freedom to differ widely as to their conception of need has led to inconsistencies of treatment between patients and to the allocation, without challenge, of scarce resources to medical practices of no proven value. It is by no means clear that it is the patient who gains from clinical freedom. The doctor stands in the rather unique position of being both a supplier and an arbitrator. This gives him enormous discretion. It has survived largely as a consequence of a widespread view that sickness is an unambiguous state which, following diagnosis, suggests a standard and self-evident treatment which would attract universal agreement from a profession composed of individuals of high but largely homogeneous talent.

The truth is that consultants and general practitioners differ as much as any other group of graduates. Some are brilliant, some indifferent and some incompetent. Some are industrious and some indolent. How does the patient monitor the doctor? How does he become aware of the input possibilities? The leech bottle managed to survive the First World War in some British hospitals. In the absence of clinical freedom, would unavoidable rationing take place more rationally, consistently and efficiently to the mutual benefit of taxpayer and patient? Certainly such heroic individualism is inconsistent with modern management.

7 PLANNING AND MANAGEMENT

The misunderstanding as to the nature of need has resulted in little or no effective planning and control. Research into various aspects of need has been sparse and largely uncoordinated. A visiting team from the US National Institute of Health in 1968 expressed surprise that 'despite twenty years of public control the NHS has failed to evolve an effective planning mechanism' (Bierman, 1968). The result has been the persistence of the very inequalities which the health service was, in part, formed to remove.

The central machinery for assessing the purpose, direction and priorities of the NHS has always existed but in practice has been employed only rarely. Clear cut obtainable national standards have never existed. Long term planning has emerged as the aggregation of individual regional board aspirations or as simple extrapolated trends of usage. In the words of one of the service's Chief Medical Officers planning has amounted to 'the use of last year's budget with a bit added here and a bit taken off there — we never ask ourselves the big questions' (Brotherston, 1970).

Detailed decisions about priorities have been left to doctors and the hospital authorities over which they have tended to dominate. Decisions have been based upon last year's allocation plus an incremental percentage and something extra for any service involved in public scandals. Klein has aptly called this 'fiscal blind man's buff' (Klein, 1974).

Inequalities

The persistence of regional inequalities is a case in point. It is generally acknowledged that the stock of manpower and capital which the service inherited was very unequally distributed geographically although hard evidence is at a premium. Certainly the National Health Insurance

Scheme, by omitting hospitalisation from its coverage, left the distribution of consultants virtually untouched between the two World Wars. After the Second World War some counties lacked even a single gynaecologist whilst in the Eastern Region only two hospitals could boast a psychiatrist and no thoracic surgeon or dermatologist was readily available at all (Nuffield, 1946). Again, although by 1938 the 'panel system' covered some forty per cent of the population the distribution of purchasing power exerted a strong influence upon the location of general practitioners, so that South Shields, for example, had seven times as many residents per general practitioner as Hampstead (PEP, 1944).

The inception of the National Health Service in 1948 did not bring in its wake any sweeping changes. In fact the initial allocation of resources in 1948 exactly reflected the pre-NHS imbalances. Subsequent distributions of manpower and finance have preserved them largely intact.

The newly appointed Regional Hospital Boards were instructed to assess the need for new resources and to secure 'a proper and sufficient service of all kinds for persons in their areas' (Ministry of Health, 1948). Aid by which to adjudge 'proper and sufficient' was provided by the Ministry in the form of ratios of specialists to population. These ratios proved so unrealistic that for all practical purposes they were stillborn (Stevens, 1966).

The introduction of geographically uniform rates of pay for hospital doctors and of uniform *per capita* payments for general practitioners left the relative attractiveness of practising in pleasant areas of Britain and in centres of comparative excellence largely intact. The right to treat private patients also remained as a further inducement to practise in these same areas.

Attempts to rationalise the distribution of general practitioners by a system of negative direction involving the closing of adequately doctored areas to newcomers met with some success as long as the supply of newcomers continued to expand. With the decline in numbers however the more unfashionable and already under-doctored areas suffered most. The percentage of population living in areas officially designated as under-doctored fell from fifty-two per cent in 1952 to

61

seventeen per cent in 1961. Between 1963-7, however, this percentage rose, with the decline in general practitioner numbers, to thirty-eight per cent, but it is now dropping again and is currently standing at thirty-four per cent. Faced with the rapid re-emergence of the problem in 1966 financial inducements were introduced.

Executive Councils can 'designate' any area which after nominally allocating 2,500 patients to each available doctor, has at least 2,500 left over (i.e. the area is one or more doctors short). This, of course, ignores the *actual* distribution of list sizes in the area, so that the character and size of designated areas varies a good deal in practice. New doctors to such an area receive an initial grant and an annual supplement of between £490 and £700 depending upon the gravity of the local situation. When an area has been designated for three years, all the doctors receive the supplement irrespective of their actual list sizes (only one year in the worst areas). Further, if an area ceases to be designated, the supplement continues for three years. In practice this scheme has had little effect. First, the size of the supplement is likely to be only about ten per cent of the doctor's expected income and second, doctors tend to work where they do for largely non-monetary reasons. The more links a doctor has with a region the more likely he is to work there. In J.R. Butler's (1973) study the doctor's home area and the location of his medical school were the most important influences. In the event, twenty-five per cent of the East Midland's general practitioners have lists over 3,000 (with an average of 2,580), in contrast to the South West where the corresponding figures are only eight per cent and 2,224. Ten years ago the East Midlands were slightly better off than now with twenty per cent of the lists over 3,000 and the South West was slightly worse off with nine per cent.

Additions to the stock of hospital doctors have simply reflected the existing distribution. Areas likely to attract new staff are clearly the most likely to advertise new posts. There has been no positive attempt at direction from the centre or any inducements offered to attract talent to the less attractive areas. In fact, the chances of a consultant receiving a merit award are forty per cent in London and thirty-six per cent on Oxford, as against thirty per cent in Sheffield, Birmingham and

Manchester. The official inducements appear to reinforce the attractions of the availability of private practice, centres of excellence and prestige and so on which basically tend to influence the location of hospital manpower. There has been, however, some equalisation of these chances over recent years.

Defining 'area of residence' at its broadest, an attempt was made in 1966 to assess the extent of inequalities in both manpower and expenditure between the areas covered by each of the fifteen Regional Hospital Boards by constructing thirty-one indices from official sources (Cooper and Culyer, 1972). It was seen that in almost every instance the Sheffield Region appeared less well-endowed than the Oxford Region. Although frequently difficult to meaningfully interpret they raised a great number of questions which were in urgent need of an answer. Why, for example, had the Newcastle Region twice as many gynaecologists per female as Sheffield (in fact the disparity actually increased when the population at risk was adjusted by sex); why had Birmingham twice as many whole time equivalent consultants as Sheffield; why had Liverpool twice as many psychiatrists as Manchester; why did the children of Oxford have twice as many tonsillectomies as those in Sheffield and so on? In fact six indices had ranges over one hundred per cent, sixteen over fifty per cent and one had a range of over six hundred per cent.

No evidence of one variable compensating for a deficiency in another could be found. The areas relatively deprived on one yardstick were regularly deprived on another. For example, the coefficient of correlation between medical salaries per patient week and nursing salaries was 0.84; that between medical salaries and expenditure upon equipment, 0.73; and that between equipment and pharmaceuticals, 0.67. Nor was there any evidence of capital substitution for labour or vice versa.

To the extent that teaching hospitals with their superior staff-patient ratios and heavy concentrations of consultants with A+ merit rewards are centres of excellence, it could be maintained that access to their beds should also be equal irrespective of region. In fact Wessex had no such hospital beds, whilst the North Western Metropolitan Region had one bed per 615 people. Excluding Wessex and all the

Metropolitan areas, the range was from Manchester with 3,714 persons per bed to Oxford with 1,356. There is, of course, undoubtedly a case to be made for centres of excellence as such, but only if there is a rational and well-advertised set of allocation principles for patients drawn from a national catchment area. All should have equal opportunity of benefitting in accordance with some consensus of medically determined need.

In the period 1962-7 regional inequalities appeared to be increasing. The coefficient of variation for consultants per million population was fifteen per cent in 1962 and seventeen per cent in 1966 despite a twenty-two per cent increase in their total numbers. Gynaecologists and obstetricians for example increased over the period by eleven per cent but their coefficient of variation rose from seventeen per cent to nineteen per cent. Again the coefficient of variation for general practitioners rose from eighteen per cent to twenty-one per cent but this time in the face of a fall in their numbers by 2.2 per cent. Even in the case of consultants where manpower had been growing there did not appear to have been any systematic attempt to erase inequalities.

The health service had successfully dismantled the price barrier but had failed to deal with the others. Inequalities of a geographical nature are unlikely to be any more equitable than those resulting from inequalities in the distribution of purchasing power and clearly there was nothing inherent in the 1946 Act which could have systematically brought equality about. Indeed even today the data upon which to base relevant decisions remains largely lacking. By 1969 the then Minister in charge could still describe regional inequalities as the 'single most difficult problem' we face (Crossman, 1969).

There has, of course, been improvement. Table 14 shows that although Sheffield remained bottom of the revenue league in 1971-2, as a percentage of the best region, Sheffield improved her position from only forty-nine per cent in 1950-1 to seventy-five per cent in 1971-2. The greatest variations, however, are still found in the manpower ratios. Hospital medical and dental staff *per capita* in Sheffield remained only fifty-eight per cent of those in the metropolitan regions and nurses only seventy-one per cent of those in Liverpool. General

TABLE 14 Regional Hospital Boards – England

Revenue Allocation per Head of Population
Table by the Department of Health and Social Security

Regional Hospital Board	1950-1		1971-2	
	Allocation per head of population	Percentage of National average for RHB hospitals	Allocation per head of population	Percentage of National average for RHB hospitals
	£		£	
England	4.3	100	19.7	100
Newcastle	3.6	83	19.6	99
Leeds	3.8	89	21.0	107
Sheffield	3.0	71	16.6	84
East Anglia	3.5	82	16.9	86
N.W. Metropolitan	5.3	123	18.7	95
N.E. Metropolitan	5.7	134	21.6	110
S.E. Metropolitan	5.8	135	20.8	106
S.W. Metropolitan and Wessex	6.1	143	22.1	112
Oxford	3.7	86	17.5	89
South Western	4.4	103	20.9	106
Birmingham	3.4	80	18.0	91
Manchester	3.3	78	19.8	101
Liverpool	4.2	98	21.6	110

Notes: The figures take no account of the cost of services carried out by Boards of Governors of teaching hospitals.
S.W. Metropolitan and Wessex were not separate regions in 1950-1.

Source: Expenditure Committee (Public Expenditure Sub-Committee), Appendix 4, Minutes of Evidence, 1972.

practitioners and dentists varied between the regions by sixteen per cent and eighty-seven per cent respectively in contrast to nineteen per cent and ninety-eight per cent ten years ago. Beds *per capita* range by seventy-five per cent between Sheffield and the South Western Metropolitan Region compared with eighty-four per cent ten years ago. In Manchester, each consultant has 74.7 persons waiting on the list for admission, whilst in the South Western Metropolitan Region the figure is only 28.6. *Per capita* the waiting list varied from over fourteen per thousand to 8.5 (Table 15). In 1973 medical pay per inpatient week varied between regional boards by forty-two per cent, nurses pay by twenty-four per cent, drug expenditure by forty per cent and catering by twenty-eight per cent for nonteaching hospitals of one hundred beds or more.

TABLE 15 Regional waiting lists in England and Wales in 1971.

Regional Hospital Board	list per 1,000 population	list per consultant	size of list
South Western	14.3	66.1	45,334
Manchester	14.2	74.7	65,101
N.W. Metropolitan	12.3	28.4	52,194
Birmingham	11.9	59.2	60,774
Oxford	11.8	51.0	23,602
Wales	11.8	60.2	32,161
Sheffield	10.5	64.8	48,725
S.E. Metropolitan	10.3	35.8	35,170
Newcastle	10.2	43.4	31,021
Liverpool	9.7	34.9	21.424
N.E. Metropolitan	9.5	33.7	30,911
Wessex	8.9	47.5	18,191
S.W. Metropolitan	8.5	26.6	28,668
East Anglia	8.5	38.5	15,058
Leeds	7.0	34.9	22,586

Source: A.J. Culyer and J.G. Cullis, *New Society*, 16 August 1973.

Clearly there is no way of saying from all these figures of variation which level of provision is in some sense correct. Do relatively low figures for Sheffield suggest great efficiency or deprivation? By Liverpool's standards, Sheffield needs another nine thousand nurses. Do the figures for Oxford suggest adequacy or waste? Rather it is more likely that both sets of figures simply indicate the *vagueness* of the concept of medical adequacy. Need expands to meet whatever resources are provided. There are certainly no obvious signs of deprivation in Sheffield and if all regions were brought into line with the levels of provision enjoyed by Oxford and the Metropolitan regions the cost implication for the NHS would be very large indeed.

There is, of course, no particular virtue in the equality of provision as such. Need is most unlikely to be equal throughout the country. In the absence, however, of any reliable or accepted indicator of need, *per capita* equality would appear a more rational goal than the perpetuation of historical chance. In fact current provision appears to bear an almost inverse relationship to need as indicated by crude mortality and morbidity statistics.

Exeter, which is very well endowed with doctors, has a local adjusted death rate to national death rate ratio of only 0.90 compared with, say, Rhondda's 1.36 or Preston's 1.29. Again Oxfordshire with 0.85 can be contrasted with Durham's 1.17 or Glamorgan's 1.20. Oxford's infant mortality rate of fifteen per thousand contrasts with Sheffield's 18.3 per thousand. Morbidity as reflected in sickness certificates (albeit very poorly) shows the Welsh to have had 30.5 days of incapacity per man at risk in 1968-9 compared with only 10.7 in the South East (Whitehead, 1971). Of course these variations reflect standard of living, unemployment rates and a multitude of other variables but there is clearly no systematic relation to health care provision.

A survey by Logan and his colleagues (1972) attempted to test two hypotheses with respect to the current provision of resources. The first was that provision reflected need and the second was that variations in provision compensated for weaknesses in the other social services (community and welfare). The study was carried out in the Liverpool region where provision ratios are for the most part above the average (with higher expenditure, manpower and admission rates and longer stays). Neither hypothesis stood up to testing. Services provided always generated the need necessary to fully utilise them. Extra bed availability resulted in the admission of less severe cases and the longer retention of patients already in hospital. No good explanations for Liverpool's relatively high consumption of resources could be found in this very extensive and professional piece of research.

Another form of variation is in expenditure between categories of hospital and patients (Table 16). Bed week costs in 1973 varied from £28.02 for the mentally handicapped (less in fact than it costs to keep a man in prison!) to £89.00 for acute hospitals and £129.14 for London teaching hospitals. These differences were reflected in even the nonmedical costs. Catering costs varied from £3.58 a week for the mentally handicapped to £12.68 in the London teaching hospitals. Such differences cannot be explained by variations in medical dietary needs.

TABLE 16   Average Inpatient Costs per week by Type of Hospital (England)

	Total Inpatient Cost			Medical Costs	Nursing Costs	Catering Costs
	1971	1972	1973	1973	1973	1973
All Acute	65.13	76.56	89.06	5.32	24.72	8.18
Teaching Hospitals						
London	97.74	112.25	129.14	7.64	28.34	12.68
Provincial	87.84	99.53	115.66	7.55	24.50	10.61
Mental Illness	21.39	25.45	30.34	1.42	11.30	3.77
Mental Handicap	18.86	23.39	28.02	0.73	10.14	3.58
Long Stay	29.68	34.86	40.25	1.42	15.98	4.54

Source: Hospital Costing Returns, 31 March 1973.

Nevertheless, these figures do show some slight improvement since 1971 in that mental illness and handicap inpatient costs have increased from thirty-three per cent to thirty-four per cent and from twenty-nine per cent to thirty-two per cent respectively of the acute hospital expenditure. The comparable figure for expenditure in the long stay hospitals is forty-five per cent but this has changed very little in the past ten years or more.

TABLE 17 Geriatric and Chronic Sick Beds (England)
Table by the Department of Health and Social Security

	1961		1970	
	Beds available	Percentage of National Average. Ratio of beds to elderly population	Beds available	Percentage of National Average. Ratio of beds to elderly population
England	53,901	100	57,205	100
Regions:				
Newcastle	2,937	87	3,532	101
Leeds	5,125	139	5,294	129
Sheffield	4,940	95	5,293	100
East Anglia	2,592	128	2,395	101
N.W. Metropolitan	3,246	60	3,586	78
N.E. Metropolitan	3,950	94	4,193	104
S.E. Metropolitan	4,258	98	4,347	83
S.W. Metropolitan	2,919	70	3,460	78
Oxford	2,268	105	2,370	107
South Western	4,755	117	5,051	110
Birmingham	6,166	119	6,315	116
Manchester	5,996	109	6,141	105
Liverpool	2,489	109	2,605	104
Wessex	2,263	98	2,623	89

Source: As for Table 14.

Provision of beds for the geriatric and long stay patients also shows considerable variation between the regions. Table 17 shows that whilst the situation is improving the worst provided region was still only sixty per cent of the best in beds per elderly person at risk. In 1971 beds available for mental illness *per capita* varied by 179 per cent and those for the mentally handicapped by two hundred per cent. Further, the ratio of staff to patients between mental illness hospitals of two hundred beds or more varied for all medical staff from 0.55 to 8.66 per hundred patients. Psychiatrists varied, somewhat incredibly, from 0.15 to 3.36, nurses from 22.50 to 70.90 and domestic staff from 0.50 to 17.90 per hundred patients. Despite these extraordinary variations there was evidence of improvement since 1964 when eighty-two per cent of patients resident in hospitals of five hundred beds or more had consultant to patient ratios of less than 0.45 per hundred. By 1971 this had fallen to fifty-five per cent of patients (Bransby, 1973). In 1972 the Department of Health set some long overdue minimum standards, the target for their achievement being 1974. These were what was considered to be practical within the limits of manpower and not what was considered *desirable*.

The regional disparities have also been recognised by the NHS. Richard Crossman (1969) saw them as so big that there was no easy way of aiding 'underprivileged areas with a major legitimate grievance' without cutting back on the more favoured areas. In this Crossman was echoing the sentiments of Enoch Powell three years earlier, who referred to the 'political odium of being seen to reduce expenditure' (Powell, 1966). Nonetheless during his period of office considerable attention was given to formulating standards towards which all regions should move.

Until 1971, however, no explicit effort was made to allocate resources to Regional Hospital Boards on the basis of a need formula. 'We had not developed any acceptable system of measuring the relative needs of regions' according to the then Under-Secretary of State for Health (Alison, 1972). A year later he told the House of Commons that 'at present we have neither a comprehensive assessment of need, nor a thorough going audit, as it were, of the existing stock' (Alison, 1973). The current formula is based fairly crudely upon population weighted by age and sex, cases treated, and the current supply of beds. Each of the following factors is used to determine the theoretical allocation for each individual region.

(a)   Population: the national total revenue moneys are divided in direct proportion to the weighted populations served in each region.

(b)   Beds grouped under specialities are multiplied by annual costs of providing hospital services based on national average costs per inpatient week (similarly for outpatient attendances).

(c)   Cases (inpatients and outpatients) by specialities are multiplied by the appropriate national average costs of treating a case.

Then, a combined theoretical allocation is derived by adding one half of the population based allocation and one quarter of each of the other two calculated figures and making a few adjustments for such factors as higher rates of pay in the London area. Equality under the formula is to take place gradually over the next ten years. Although the formula can be criticised for having the effect of diverting funds to the efficient (West, 1973) and hence, in a way, increasing their relative advantages, it is an explicit attempt at rationality and is to be applauded. It needs the backing of some positive discrimination, however, in the form of higher pay for consultants and others willing to work in unfashionable geographical areas and in specialities such as child psychiatry, venerology and radiology and considerably larger general practice inducements than those currently offered.

Planning and management have been weak mainly because of clinical freedom. Central pronouncements of priorities are statements of faith when it is doctors who have the final say at the point of delivery. The problem of allocating more funds to the elderly illustrates the point clearly: the Department of Health and Social Security told the Expenditure Committee that 'the existence of clinical freedom substantially reduces the ability of the central authority to determine objectives and priorities and to control individual facets of expenditure' (DHSS evidence to Expenditure Committee, 1971). It is the doctor who, in the final analysis, decides whether to treat a patient of a given type or not. 'It is not possible to estimate what proportion of the additional resources will be devoted specifically to accommodation for the elderly. . . This is partly because the financial returns relate to services, not users, and also because decisions on priorities are made by the relevant administering authorities at the local level.' The Hospital Advisory Service gives some indication of what happens at the local level. It reported in the same year that 'it is still usual to find that new hospitals are being planned with far too few geriatric beds on the assumption that the geriatricians and the other staff will be content to take over old and inconvenient premises vacated by other specialists' (Hospital Advisory Service, 1972).

If the centre could not direct resources and manpower it could at least have offered incentives towards the desired end. In the event, however, merit awards are still six times greater in neuro-surgery than in geriatrics (Lavers, 1972). Further, central policy has little hope of implementation unless the criteria of success is spelt out clearly and the data made available to test it.

Management Problems and the New Administrative Structure

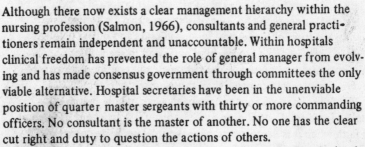

Although there now exists a clear management hierarchy within the nursing profession (Salmon, 1966), consultants and general practitioners remain independent and unaccountable. Within hospitals clinical freedom has prevented the role of general manager from evolving and has made consensus government through committees the only viable alternative. Hospital secretaries have been in the unenviable position of quarter master sergeants with thirty or more commanding officers. No consultant is the master of another. No one has the clear cut right and duty to question the actions of others.

The lack of normal chains of management has resulted in the kinds of misallocation of resources within hospitals reported by Logan *et al* (1972). His team found, for example, that the allocation of beds between consultants was seriously out of line with their respective requirements and with their theatre time. Beatrice Hunter (1972) reported in her study that patients were admitted on set days irrespective of the amount of preparation needed, thus wasting inpatients time. Even in strictly nonmedical areas the health service's efficiency has been seriously questioned. The service is in effect Britain's largest hotel and laundry chain. One quarter of the total hospital budget goes upon supplies and equipment, mostly in common use. Suppliers, however, complain of irregular and unplanned purchases, duplicated orders and having to deal with several departments within one management committee area (OHE, 1972). The Public Accounts Committee (1972), the Parliamentary watchdog over public spending, complains of failures to select the cheapest gas and electricity tariffs and of small scale purchases of even the more common user goods. There is clearly 'scope for economy in the use of resources within the framework of existing assumptions and practice' (Logan, 1972).

Despite Logan involving medical personnel at all stages in his work, his team found considerable professional resistance to any proposals for reform however small. As Claudine McCreadie (1974) commented in reviewing his work, 'the battle for efficiency in health services is surely at root a battle about who is to control the activities of professions and how.'

In April 1974 the NHS was radically reorganised (Figures 4 and 5). Great hopes for the new structure have been expressed in terms of the introduction of modern management techniques. Formidable barriers exist, however, in the form of tradition, emotion and professional self-interest and it is these which will finally determine how the legislature's intent is translated into practice. In the event, the reorganisation may prove to be little more than the illusion of change.

The new organisation has been much influenced by the advice given to the authorities by McKinsey and Company, a firm of consultants. The result is that some six thousand regional, hospital management and executive council committee members have been replaced with 1,600 in a more unified system. The new smaller committees are to be managerial rather than somewhat ambiguously representative. Supported by permanent staff and professional committees they will have a duty to appraise, adjudicate and make explicit rationing decisions.

The basic operational units are 205 Health Districts each serving approximately a quarter million population each. These have a management team of six persons (a specialist, general practitioner, nurse, community physician, administrator and financial advisor). Their task is to manage and coordinate, reviewing needs and deciding priorities

73

FIGURE 4

The NHS Structure 1948-74

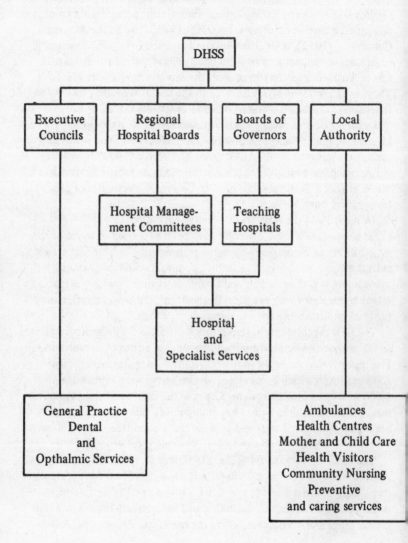

The NHS Structure from 1 April 1974

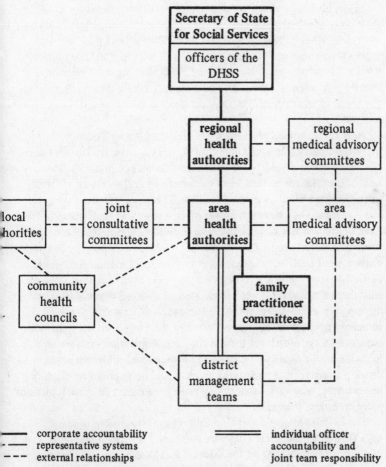

—— corporate accountability	══ individual officer
– · — representative systems	accountability and
– – – external relationships	joint team responsibility

ce: *Management Arrangements for the Reorganized NHS*, HMSO 1972

in the light of those needs. Essentially their management task is concerned with the day to day running of the health system. The concept of a chief executive is firmly rejected. Teams are 'groups of equals, no member being the managerial superior of another.' The role of the two medical committee members, for example, is to represent the consensus view of their colleagues or 'to express views when they have, or that is reasonably likely that they will be able to obtain, the support of their colleagues' (HMSO, 1972). They alone on the committee will be elected by their colleagues working in the district and they will also serve as chairman and vice-chairman of a district medical committee, itself a representative forum for local medical opinions. The community physician is intended to be a planner taking an over-view of all the needs of the district. He has, however, no executive authority over medical staff.

Also at the district level there are Health Planning Teams to investigate particular needs and groups, and Community Health Councils which are intended to articulate the consumers' interests. The task of the CHCs is to feed back local opinion and to act as 'visitors' to the health amenities in their locality. These councils have tongues but no teeth. They have the power merely to report their views to the Area Board and not to take any action. Neither are they elected. Rather twenty to thirty people emerge out of the shadows, upon the mysterious say so of local authorities, voluntary associations and the health authorities themselves. Although no provision exists for this, presumably these Councils will need some kind of national organisation and meeting place if they are to profit from each other's experiences and to make known their opinions. Certainly they will need the help and guidance of a professional team if they are to question matters as technical as the quality of care or the professional priorities in their district. Considerable back room work would be required to question, for example, why certain mortality rates were higher or cross infections more common, than elsewhere.

The District Management Committees are responsible to ninety Area Health Authorities. These are composed of fifteen members, four of whom are appointed by the relevant local authority and the remainder by the regional board. The Chairman is the nominee of the

Secretary for State and is paid. In order to facilitate coordination and integration with local government services, the AHA's boundaries exactly coincide with those of the new local government authorities. This is, of course, of particular importance for the elderly, children and the handicapped who need social and community aid related to and integrated with health care provision. Joint consultative committees have been formed in the attempt to ensure that such integration takes place.

The AHA committees 'will decide guidelines on priorities and available resources, review and challenge objectives, plans and budgets' and resolve competing claims between districts. They are also to monitor progress and take 'appropriate action to correct any unsatisfactory performance.' There is a considerable variation in the size of the AHA areas. One third of them have only one district whilst others up to five. Five of them cover populations in excess of one million, fifteen populations under a quarter million (Table 18).

Immediately answerable to the Department of Health and Social Security and above the AHAs, are fourteen Regional Health Authorities with, for the most part, the same boundaries as the old Regional Hospital Boards. These have about fifteen to twenty voluntary members, all nominated by the Secretary of State. These are responsible for 'important issues of policy, planning and resource allocation' and for monitoring the performance of the AHAs. They are also responsible for major capital projects and for the Blood Transfusion Service.

The reorganisation is obviously a compromise representing hardly anyone's ideal. The need to align boundaries with the new Local Authorities has given rise to the 'area.' There are too many areas to be directly controlled and they are in any case too small for planning units but too large for health catchment areas. Thus the district area is needed, centred on the district general hospital and community services. Unfortunately the health districts do not always reflect local authority social service management units. Whilst the health districts cover 80,000 to 450,000 people, the social teams operate on the basis of fifty thousand to one hundred thousand people.

The other major new committee is the Family Practitioner

TABLE 18 Variations in Regional and Area Authority Size

Regions	Population (1,000s)	Nos of areas	Nos of areas in population brackets (1000s)				
			under 250	250-500	500-750	750-1000	over 1000
West Midlands	5,119	11	1	7	1	1	1
Trent	4,469	8	2	1	2	3	-
North Western	4,075	11	5	4	1	-	1
Yorkshire	3,568	7	1	3	2	1	-
Northern	3,139	9	3	4	2	-	-
South Western	3,045	5	-	3	-	2	-
Wessex	2,541	3	-	1	1	-	1
Mersey	2,518	6	2	2	1	1	-
Oxford	2,098	4	-	2	2	-	-
East Anglia	1,681	3	-	-	3	-	-
North East Thames	3,767	6	-	3	2	-	1
South East Thames	3,630	5	-	2	1	1	1
South West Thames	2,902	5	-	2	1	2	-
North West Thames	3,539	7	1	4	1	1	-
Total	46,090	90	15	38	20	12	5

Committee. This is basically a new name for the Executive Council except that each Committee covers an entire health area. Nominally integrated with the hospital service under the AHAs, in practice it is a very autonomous body with fifty per cent professional representation and virtually no managerial control or influence over the independent contractor general practitioner and his professional colleagues. Each general practitioner remains free to exercise his own judgment over, for example, at least £8,500 of medicines, subject only to a visit every other year or so from his regional medical officer who, in the course of wide ranging discussions, can call attention to his prescribing habits if they are seriously out of line with the average for the area. In practice this forms only some five per cent of regional medical officers' workload.

The hope for this new system is that it improves the *capacity* of the NHS for improvement. It is not a once and for all change but simply the first step towards explicit monitoring (however vague the processes and methods of scrutiny as currently suggested), integrated management, evaluation and planning. It will be a long struggle. At present the data does not exist. What the new system inherits is a mountain of data untouched by the human brain (Chester, 1973). The fear is that professional self-interest will finally convert the initiative into nothing more than one form of fragmentation replaced by another. A structure which depends upon consensus government is going to find it difficult to encourage any new managerial virtues. It seems unlikely that the medical profession suddenly will discover a capacity for unanimity. Indeed the new structure may fail to satisfy both those demanding more rational and explicit line management and those hoping for greater decentralisation and democratisation.

Perhaps the greatest problem with the new system is the failure (with the exception of Northern Ireland) to include the personal social services under its umbrella. The acutely ill, if they are to have ever shorter periods of hospital stay, clearly need coordinated community support whilst the elderly and handicapped need very close liason between the services if they are not to be unnecessarily hospitalised (Brown, 1973).

The new administration will, of course, take over much of the old. Perhaps most interesting is the likely future of the 'Cogwheel' committees. These committees, where they exist (for in Sheffield and Liverpool a majority of hospitals still lack them), represent a meeting of all consultants within one hospital. The original intention was to try and involve consultants in management so that they became more aware of the probable financial implications of their actions. According to Klein (1971) each consultant is responsible for spending something in excess of £120,000 a year.

The latest (and third) report of the Joint Working Party on the Organisation of Medical Work in Hospitals (1974) emphasises the possible role of these Cogwheel Committees in reviewing the effectiveness and quality of medical care. Self-criticism could take place, in the form of reviews of current practices, anaesthetic mortalities and so on. In their own words, 'The working party does not believe that standard patterns of treatment or investigation should be imposed . . . It does believe, however, that in many circumstances the *individual clinician needs to have regard to the collective view of his colleagues on best current practice in particular situations*' [my italics]. In other words if a consultant persistently uses eccentric volumes of resources in the form of bed rest, X-rays, blood transfusing and so on, he should come under the collective pressure of his colleagues.

The report is most encouraging and mirrors what the present author and others have been urging for some years. Whether, even if it became universally and fully implemented, it would prove sufficient, is more doubtful. What is basically at fault is the complete freedom of each consultant and his 'firm' to go his own way within a plethora of small units. Can collective pressure really be marshalled and made effective in the absence of a 'Chief Consultant' figure? One area in which an experiment in quality monitoring has been carried out is maternity. Inquests have been conducted into deaths due to pregnancy and childbirth to see whether any lapses from the expected standards of care could be detected. The report for England and Wales concluded that fifty-six per cent of these deaths had 'avoidable factors' (HMSO, 1972), whilst that for Scotland estimated that one third of the deaths were avoidable and that in half of these doctors were wholly or partly responsible. Delays in diagnosis, failure to call in expert advice and inadequate follow-up were the most recurrent mistakes made by doctors (HMSO, 1974).

Under the new system the strictly hierarchical nursing profession will continue to be 'coordinated' with the representatives of the hospital doctors. Consultants are not of homogeneous talent. They vary in ability and intellect as much as any other group of graduates. The competent but undistinguished might benefit from the guidance, encouragement and shared responsibility which comes with more hierarchical professional structures. The incompetent and indolent need the exposure and accountability of line management. All would probably profit from the incentive offered by the prospect of further advancement above the rank of consultant. The medical profession, however, claims that management is inconsistent with good medicine. Undoubtedly the present system is perfectly consistent with bad medicine. The profession dominates current management whilst at the same time rejecting it.

8 THE FUTURE

Finance

The uniqueness of the NHS is one of degree rather than of kind. There is, for example, no national health system which is entirely free of state finance. The highest proportion of private (non-tax) finance is found in the USA but even there direct tax subsidies combined with various tax reliefs still amount to over forty per cent of health expenditures. In Switzerland the split is of the order of 50/50 whilst at the other end of the spectrum, Sweden and New Zealand are the nearest to the British position with only twenty per cent private payments as against the British five per cent.

The essence of the British system lies in the smallness of its direct charges and in its universal coverage (although some four per cent of the population consume private medicine they remain eligible to use the NHS any time they may wish — it is not possible to 'opt out'). Any attempt to fundamentally change the system of financing away from taxation would completely undermine the system, as it is at present conceived. Nevertheless such proposals have been frequently made.

The British Medical Association's Advisory Panel on *Health Services Financing* (1970) concluded in their mammoth report that 'so long as the present financial structure of the NHS is maintained the Government must either impose further considerable increases in taxation or face a deterioration in the standard of medical care which it provides for the British people.' It continued, 'there is a limit to the level of taxation which is either acceptable to the people or compatible with a sound national economy.' They provided no guidance, however, as to how to recognise such a level or as to whether it had been reached. British taxation is, in fact, in no way exceptional by European standards, and, historically, every increase in tax has been hailed as representing the limit of public endurance. The main case for dismantling the present tax-financed health system rests on the so-called 'tax illusion.' The public tend to see little or no connection between the payment of taxes and the consumption of public goods and services. Indeed, the argument runs, they regard the payment of tax as little more than a confiscation and are, therefore, very reluctant to pay. The supply of health care is currently dependent upon the public willingness to substitute the payment of tax for direct command over private goods and services. Therefore, it is argued, if health were placed in the private rather than the public sector, people would be more willing to direct resources to it.

It may well be that people are more willing to spend their money when they can see an immediate and obvious return in the form of benefits. The present NHS, however, demands a pooling of risks and a transfer of purchasing power from the fit to the sick, from the rich to the poor, from the wage earner to the young and retired and so on. Increasing the non-tax element decreases all these other features of the system.

Interestingly enough, the Government Social Survey found that sixty per cent of the public considered that the entire cost of the NHS was met, not from general taxes, but from the weekly national insurance contribution (the insurance stamp). In practice this amounted in 1972 to only 24.1p per week per adult male worker, one third of which was paid by employers on the employee's behalf. This represents only 8½ per cent of the total cost of the NHS (Table 19). It is therefore small wonder that the public think the NHS a good bargain! The public appear equally confused as to how much tax they are in practice paying. C.V. Brown (1968) has shown in his study of standard taxpayers that no worker and only six per cent of managers were aware of their marginal rates of tax. A clear majority of both thought it to be higher than in reality, whilst twenty per cent assumed it to exceed fifty per cent (as against the true thirty-three per cent).

The BMA report (1970) proposed a reduction of fifty per cent in the health services financed by taxation, the remainder to be financed privately through an extensive range of charges. These charges were to be backed either by private insurance schemes or, for those unwilling to pay the premiums, a compulsory state run insurance scheme. The tax financed half of the proposed health service would cover such services as the geriatric, chronic, mentally ill and subnormal (also, somewhat curiously, the pharmaceutical services). In the event the report won few friends but many enemies and was quickly given a burial by its own sponsors.

Much of the report was sound and important (to reveal an interest the present author was a contributor to the evidence but not to the recommendations!). It rightly concluded that 'the NHS has never since the early days been able to fully cope with the rising demands that it, and the parallel development of new methods of treatment, were responsible for stimulating.' It is important, however, not to swing from the finding that the NHS has been less than utopian to the advocacy of some other system which may prove to be a good deal worse in practice.

There are five basic reasons why large scale fundamental changes in the system of finance are undesirable and hopefully unlikely to take place in the forseeable future:

i) The degree of medical risk varies very widely between individuals. The risks are of a much greater order than those associated with theft or fire. It can be more catastrophic when it strikes. Those persons with the higher health risks would have to be compulsorily admitted by all insurance companies equally. Otherwise a company which accepted bad risks on the same terms as its other business would find its premiums forced up, driving its better risks to other companies, finally driving its own premiums up still higher.

ii) The present State monopoly would break up. The NHS as the sole purchaser of medical talent and supplies has used its power to hold costs down. The service is probably one of the cheapest in the world. We have, for example, the lowest drug prices in Europe (Cooper, 1972). Insurance companies on the other hand, would become little more than bill payers, automatically adjusting premiums to risks and leaving patients to increase their coverage in line

TABLE 19   National Health and Welfare Services: Sources of Finance
(Great Britain)

Source	Unit	1958-9	1963-4	1964-5	1965-6	1966-7	1967-8	1968-9	1969-70	1970-1	1971-2
All Services	£ million	803	1,147	1,254	1,389	1,520	1,669	1,793	1,952	2,369	2,698
	Per cent	*100*	*100*	*100*	*100*	*100*	*100*	*100*	*100*	*100*	*100*
Central Government Services	£ million	707	995	1,088	1,201	1,313	1,435	1,537	1,685	1,968	2,217
	Per cent	*88.0*	*86.7*	*86.8*	*86.5*	*86.4*	*86.0*	*85.7*	*86.3*	*83.1*	*82.2*
Consolidated Fund	£ million	568	775	866	1,007	1,114	1,241	1,304	1,447	1,688	1,900
	Per cent	*70.7*	*67.5*	*69.1*	*72.5*	*73.3*	*74.4*	*72.7*	*74.1*	*71.3*	*70.4*
Insurance Stamp contributions	£ million	102	163	163	160	163	157	181	175	213	228
	Per cent	*12.7*	*14.2*	*13.0*	*11.5*	*10.7*	*9.4*	*10.1*	*9.0*	*9.0*	*8.5*
Charges to recipients	£ million	35	54	55	31	32	33	47	59	62	79
	Per cent	*4.4*	*4.7*	*4.4*	*2.3*	*2.1*	*2.0*	*2.6*	*3.0*	*2.6*	*2.9*
Miscellaneous	£ million	2	3	4	3	4	4	5	4	5	10
	Per cent	*0.2*	*0.3*	*0.3*	*0.2*	*0.3*	*0.2*	*0.3*	*0.2*	*0.2*	*0.4*
Local Authority Services	£ million	96	152	166	188	207	234	256	267	401	481
	Per cent	*12.0*	*13.3*	*13.2*	*13.5*	*13.6*	*14.0*	*14.3*	*13.7*	*16.9*	*17.6*
Rates and Consolidated Fund grants	£ million	83	131	143	161	179	204	223	233	356	429
	Per cent	*10.4*	*11.4*	*11.4*	*11.6*	*11.8*	*12.2*	*12.4*	*11.9*	*15.0*	*15.9*
Charges to recipients	£ million	13	21	23	27	28	30	33	34	45	52
	Per cent	*1.6*	*1.9*	*1.8*	*1.9*	*1.8*	*1.8*	*1.9*	*1.8*	*1.9*	*1.9*

Source: *Health and Personal Social Services Statistics, 1973.*

with inflationary price and wage increases. Thus, the State's leverage would be missing under an insurance system.

iii)   The danger is that an insurance system would result in more expenditure but less real resources. It is true that the tax illusion would vanish but there may well be an insurance illusion to match it! In the USA, for example, health professionals frequently despair at the failure of Americans to adequately invest in their own health insurance protection. People notoriously discount the future at absurdly high rates. Any insurance broker can provide ample evidence of inadequate fire cover, etc. As with tax, no immediate connection between payment and benefit is present and indeed, once the premium has been paid, the same moral hazards are present (up to the individual's limit of cover). It is often overlooked by the advocates of insurance based schemes that insurance and tax are merely two pipelines running off the same well (GNP). The overall constraint is the same in both cases (i.e. national income and wealth).

iv)   The argument that an insurance system would promote greater efficiency is also far from convincing. The efficiency of the service is largely producer determined. Numbers and types of hospital admission and length of stay are not determined by patients but by doctors. Nor is there evidence that insurance, even with only partial reimbursement, would discourage 'trivial' visits to the doctor. Indeed the very act of payment might make patients less guilty about it, actually increasing the incidence of such calls. In any case, what is a 'trivial' ailment? A face blemish on a model, a stomach upset two hours before an exam or desperate loneliness in a bereaved widow? What is trivial to the doctor may be a crisis to the patient. If such cases were diverted from the surgery, where would they go?

v)   Finally, an additional problem encountered by the partial type of scheme advocated by the BMA Advisory Panel is that it would remove the articulate and informed from the State Scheme leaving those, like the mentally ill and aged, to fend for themselves.

Much more likely than any such major change is the gradual expansion

TABLE 20

Charges to persons using the services (Great Britain)

Period	All services £m	Hospital £m	Pharma-ceutical £m	General dental £m	General opthalmic £m	Welfare foods £m	Local health £m	Local welfare £m	Personal social services £m
					Services				
1958-9	48	6	12	9	6	2	3	10	-
1963-4	75	8	24	12	8	2	5	16	-
1964-5	78	9	24	12	8	2	6	17	-
1965-6	58	8	-	12	9	2	7	20	-
1966-7	60	8	-	13	9	2	7	21	-
1967-8	63	9	-	13	9	2	8	22	-
1968-9	80	10	11	15	9	2	7	26	-
1969-70	93	12	18	17	10	2	7	27	-
1970-1	107	12	18	19	12	1	3	-	42
1971-2	131	15	24	25	14	1	3	-	49

Source: *Health and Personal Social Statistics, 1973.*

TABLE 21

Number and Cost of Prescriptions

England and Wales	Number of prescriptions (thousands)	Total Cost £ thousands	Net ingredient cost £ thousands	Average cost per prescription		Persons on NHS prescribing lists (thousands)	Average per person on list	
				Total Cost £	Net ingredient cost £		Prescriptions Number	Net ingredient cost £
1949	202,011	30,331	13,818	0.150	0.068	-	-	-
1959	214,029	72,908	46,689	0.341	0.218	42,593	5.03	1.096
1965	244,346	126,004	86,339	0.516	0.353	45,679	5.35	1.890
1966	261,954	138,369	95,817	0.528	0.366	46,115	5.68	2.078
1967	271,206	146,201	103,670	0.539	0.382	46,476	5.84	2.231
1968	267,378	151,667	110,314	0.567	0.413	46,863	5.71	2.354
1969	264,172	163,226	121,166	0.618	0.459	47,177	5.60	2.568
1970	266,581	179,923	133,302	0.675	0.500	47,354	5.63	2.815
1971	266,476	201,932	148,340	0.758	0.557	47,644	5.59	3.114
1972	275,820	277,388	167,842	0.824	0.610	47,858	5.75	3.507
England								
1971	247,456	187,031	137,290	0.756	0.555	45,009	5.50	3.050
1972	256,258	210,709	155,423	0.822	0.607	45,213	5.67	3.438

Source: *Health and Personal Social Services Statistics*, 1973.

of less and less 'nominal' user charges (Table 20). To date, however, charges form a more or less steady percentage of total revenues (around five per cent) although currently they are increasing slightly. In fact quite substantial charges are needed to raise even very modest revenues because of the very large number of unavoidable exemptions. Prescription charges are currently 20p per item which represents roughly one quarter of the average prescription cost (Table 21). In 1972 there were 256 million prescriptions written in England at a total cost of £211 million. Of these, 150 million prescriptions were exempt from the 20p charge.

In 1971-2 dental charges amounted to £25 million which was raised by a charge of fifty per cent of the actual cost, up to a limit of £10. Opthalmic charges consist, in the main, of a full cost charge on lenses up to a maximum of £3.50. Both charges are subject to the usual list of exemptions. There seems no very good reason for these rather odd variations between the services and presumably they reflect no one's ordering of their importance?

Since 1969 charges for visits to general practitioners, 'hotel' charges for stays in hospital, encouragement for private insurance schemes in the way of tax rebates on premiums, and prescription charges graduated up to a maximum amount, to reflect actual costs, have all been considered by the Conservative Party as candidates for official policy. None of them has come close to implementation due to the cost of collection, the list of unavoidable exemptions and the existence of a substantial 'anti' lobby. Over forty-five per cent of all occupied beds are filled by the mentally ill or mentally handicapped and forty per cent by patients over sixty-eight years old. Further, as doctors are not paid on a fee per item basis there is no obvious mechanism by which user charges could be collected.

Despite the feelings of *Pulse* (1974) that 'every GP shudders at the nightmare thought that in some future fantasy, he would be presented with a defined list of drugs, determined by a bureaucrat, from which he would compulsorily treat the patient,' a restricted list of 'free' drugs plus a more extensive one with modest user charges may not be that far off on the horizon. Certainly the probability is that pharmaceuticals will cease being a relatively stable share of the NHS bill and will begin to become an increasing one. As the relative importance of the drug bill increases, the almost complete blank cheque for prescribing enjoyed by doctors since 1948 (save for a very modest check on doctors who persistently prescribe out of line with the average for their area) is bound to be increasingly challenged. Nor is it clear why the introduction of a restriction on the range of free drugs should be 'unthinkable' to the profession but the denial of renal dialysis to patients who could clearly benefit from it be not only thinkable but current practice.

Barriers of convenience and user charges, plus the exclusion of forms of treatment from some patients altogether, do not seem any more compatible with the kind of clinical freedom sought by the medical profession than limited access by means of explicit and universally applied lists of free drugs. Restriction of service to those treatments (surgical and medical) which have the most important and well substantiated effects seems preferable to user charges which are likely to be a burden only to those least able to bear them. Certainly it is likely that to become significant sources of revenue, these charges would have to be at levels where they were also significant deterrents to demanding care and, as already stated, there exists no evidence that it is the more trivial demands that are deterred first.

Another approach would be to increase the national insurance contribution and, in particular, the share paid by the employer. This could tend to be a very regressive means of finance with even the employers' contribution in large part being passed on to consumers in higher prices. Further it would encourage the myth that the NHS is an insurance scheme. Why, in any case, should it be assumed that payment by this route is in any way preferred by the public to unearmarked taxation?

Priorities

With public revenues standing at well over forty per cent of our gross national income, disappointing growth rates, little scope for alternative sources of finance and increasing competition for a fixed pool of skilled labour, the NHS will be forced increasingly to re examine its objectives and priorities. Health expenditures cannot claim a rising proportion of our national income indefinitely and the scope for the redistribution of expenditure within the public sector must be severely limited. The NHS is likely, in fact, to be faced with a rapidly rising bill even to maintain its current levels of provision. Substantial increases in the cost of female labour (nurses alone account for thirty per cent of the bill) cannot be far off in the future. Improved work opportunities, equal pay legislation, increasing average educational attainment levels will all have their inevitable impact. Further, both consultant and general practitioner average earnings are very modest by EEC and North American standards.

Until fairly recent years, rationing has to a large extent been concentrated upon the caring rather than the curing aspects of the NHS. If the patient, in the opinion of his doctor, needed a drug, it was made available. Similarly, a patient was hospitalised (albeit often after a lengthy wait), medicated and/or operated upon. Crisis treatment of acute disorders has always been the first priority. The caring sections of the service have often appeared to be an unwanted burden which had to be tolerated but were in effect an interference in the real work of the service, namely curing the acutely ill. Translated into practice, this has meant open heart surgery rather than new central heating for the geriatric block. As a former Minister has put it, 'take my advice and do not be old or frail or mentally ill here — at least not for a few years' (Sir Keith Joseph, 1973). He might well have added, however, that it is not easy to see in which country one would be better off. Although these generalisations remain broadly true, rationing is now apparent even in the life saving departments. The most dramatic example of the explicit rationing of treatment for disorders which have an unambiguous and urgent need is to be found in the case of renal failure. There are basically three forms of treatment — diet, dialysis and transplant. The first is of value only in the mildest of cases. The current situation is that available resources have to be severely rationed amongst potential gainers so that under ten per cent of all cases and one per cent of those over fifty-five years old, are likely to receive optimal treatment. Further, within the limited number of renal dialysis units available, economic constraints have necessitated admitted reductions in hygiene standards and in patient convenience. In one unit the number of machines had to be reduced from ten to nine due to their increasing size as they became more sophisticated and less unpleasant for the patient. Nurses for these units proved to be in short supply as the demands of the unit are technologically rigorous and highly specialised. Although dialysis at night enables patients to continue at work uninterrupted, the demands of the staff have led to only daytime dialysis being provided. One of the most disturbing thirty minutes ever seen on television must have been the sight of a group of hospital staff discussing various patients' relative claims to being given access to the machines (Open University transmission, 26 April 1974). Nevertheless, such decisions appear to be unavoidable. It has been calculated, for example, that to clear the French waiting list for dialysis would cost the French the equivalent of the rest of their health expenditure (Miller, 1973). Are we, and the French, however, spending the optimal amount on fighting renal failure? Should resources be transferred from, say, tonsilectomy which achieves little, to dialysis which achieves much? Who should make such decisions and should they be made nationally or locally or where?

In fact the issue of renal dialysis is one instance in which the Department of Health and Social Security took a direct hand. 'We actually set aside a sum of money which we told the Hospital Boards should be spent on dialysis and we determined where it should be spent and how much should be spent. At that time this was a great change from our normal method of control and indeed we have hardly repeated it since.' Normally, as the Permanent Secretary of the Department put it, the difficulty in the Health Service 'is the intangible element, the difficulty of evaluating the objective or outputs to use the jargon' (Expenditure Committee, 1971).

Renal dialysis is not the only area where explicit rationing is taking place. Rosemary Briggs (1974) has drawn attention to the fact that 'ninety per cent of haemophilic patients in the UK receive less (and in some cases, much less) than optimal treatment for their complaint.' Many children are currently denied prophylactic treatment with Factor VIII to prevent pain from haemorrhage into their joints. An estimated £2 million a year would be required but is it an explicit ordering of priorities (and by whom) that denies this expenditure? Again, children in need of hole in the heart operations in the Liverpool-Warrington area have been facing a two to three year waiting list during which time they may have deteriorated to such an extent that the final outcome of the operation is affected. Although these children could have been transferred to vacancies in other regions, Liverpool doctors have had no access to any national waiting list and in any case felt they had no authority to add children to lists in other regions. In the event, instances have been reported of children being operated upon in Bordeaux rather than run the risks of the waiting period (Nationwide, 30 July 1974). Clearly a national clearing house would have made this unnecessary.

Given that medical procedures of undoubted benefit are being rationed, ought not all current practices to be rigorously tested and rejected if there is no evidence that they achieve anything positive? But what is it that the NHS is trying to achieve? As perceived by the 1946 NHS Act the objective was to 'secure improvement in the physical and mental health of the people' (p. 94). This can be expanded to preventing premature death, reducing morbidity, mitigating discomfort and alleviating the effects of disability. It is probably fair to say that although the bulk of the effort has been directed towards the first, in practice its main importance has been to the latter two.

People do not like to think about ill health. Few think of themselves as potential customers of the system. When they are customers they are too ill, and when they have recovered they are too relieved and thankful, to complain. People have notoriously high time discount rates. The present is what matters. People are unaware of what is technically possible. They have also been unaware of the gross inequalities in provision and, for the most part, have gratefully accepted whatever they have found.

Few would claim that hospitals are ideal caring environments. Discomfort starts with the ambulance ride to hospital. Essentially ambulances are adapted commercial vehicles which give poor rides, are uncomfortable on cornering and acceleration and too high from the ground to be convenient. Outpatients departments often seem to be run for the maximum convenience of consultants, whilst patients' time is valued at naught. Appointment systems which give everyone the same time still exist: the standard of comfort whilst waiting often compares unfavourably with British Rail waiting rooms. Inpatient conditions are much the same. Patients are too often treated as being uniformly stupid and afforded no privacy and little dignity. Once in bed the patient suffers an abnormal routine, with continuous anxiety-provoking activity all around him and only the barest minimum of information. These conditions can be tolerated for short spells (especially if the patient is too ill to care) but the long term patient for whom the conditions are most important ironically suffers the worst physical facilities.

Few people when fit are prepared to stay in dormitory accommodation of such a poor quality, with such a generally poor standard of food and general amenities. In 1970 twenty-seven per cent of all known cases of food poisoning occurred in hospitals — more than in restaurants, clubs, and canteens put together.

Evidence of the truth of R.M. Titmuss' (1963) warning that 'one of the new problems is the danger that the hospital may tend increasingly to be run in the interests of those working in and for the hospital rather than in the interests of the patients' is not hard to find. In practice, however, the NHS is incredibly free of patient complaints. Once hospitalised the average individual is completely submissive and hardly likely to question anything. Cartwright (1967) surveyed the attitudes of fourteen thousand patients and found 'great reluctance to criticise.' What problems they had experienced were laid typically at the door of over-work. In her earlier study (1964), Cartwright commented that patients tended to be diffident about their own position and to accept authoritarian practices in a passive and uncritical way, regarding the medical staff as inaccessible gods. Early calling, the frequency of bed making and the lack of privacy were the main concerns amongst those who felt moved to comment. Rather disturbingly, despite the government's request only forty-three per cent of hospitals include information as to the complaints procedure in their admissions booklet (Davis Report, 1973).

Of course those with the most cause for complaint have the least opportunity. The appalling story of some of the mentally handicapped institutions is now well documented (Ely, 1969; Farleigh, 1971; Whittingham, 1972). The latest committee of enquiry (Ockenham, 1974) revealed in one ward 'a wholly unacceptable and completely unjustifiable way of life.' They commented that despite the good intentions of the consultant in conditions of overcrowding and staff shortages 'we have seen in the history of this villa (ward) all the stultifying effects that can flow from an unimaginative subservience to the doctrine of the clinical autonomy of the consultant. The patients undoubtedly suffered because of it.'

Many similar fears have been expressed in the mental illness field (Harrison, 1974). Compulsory admission rates vary widely (from 143 to 330 per thousand patients) and once hospitalised, patients are in a poor position to complain however bad the conditions or treatment. Complaints can be easily dismissed as symptoms of the illness (e.g. delusions). It sometimes seems as if, to quote David Webster, secretary of the International Commission of Human Rights, 'a person who tells an inadmissable story – which seems to damage the reputation of professional colleagues is a person who is "mentally disordered" ' (quoted in Harrison, 1974). When consultants have an average of one hour per annum per patient it would be extraordinary indeed if patients did not suffer from delays in prescribing, in monitoring side effects, in over treatment and in discharge following recovery. The isolation of these patients must be removed. Why should it not be obligatory for MPs to visit at least once per annum all institutionalised persons within their constituencies? Even staff working within these institutions were ignored when they complained to the authorities.

Another factor is that the elderly patient has very low expectations of what is possible and reasonable to demand in the way of comfort and consideration whilst in hospital. The new generations may prove less uncritical. A number of surveys have shown that young patients complain much more frequently than the elderly. A survey, for example, at the Christie cancer hospital in Manchester of 453 patients revealed that the patient aged sixty-five or over complained less on every issue ranging from waking-up times to the amount of privacy with the one exception of the quantity of food served. Those under thirty-five were consistently more critical than those aged thirty-five to fifty-four, and these in turn more critical than those aged fifty-five to sixty-five (Eardly and Wakefield, 1974).

The low priority given to caring would not matter as much if the NHS was primarily life saving. Crude mortality indicators look impressive. Infant, neonatal, perinatal and maternal mortality have all fallen more than forty per cent since 1949 but the trends, particularly for overall mortality, have been flattening out. Further, much of the credit must be due to environmental and economic advances which have little to do with the NHS. Certainly international comparisons yield little support for any close correlation between expenditure upon health care resources and the actual health of the nation. The USA spends more than three times as much per head in dollar terms as the UK but with little noticeable advantage. Nor, according to some authorities, does history lend much support. Illich (1974), for example, in describing the dramatic changes in the nature of prevalent disease over the past one hundred years comes to the rather extreme conclusion that 'despite intensive research no connection between these changes in disease patterns can be attributed to the professional practice of medicine.'

Many of the NHSs triumphs have been in keeping people alive but chronically sick, and in improving the quality of life. Life expectancy at birth for males grew 2.5 years between 1948 and 1971 but declined slightly for those aged sixty or over. In fact, probably no more than ten per cent of surgery, for example, is of the emergency life or death kind (Bunker, 1974). The great bulk is an attempt to intervene (rather than cure) by making life more tolerable. In practice, however, little or anything is known as to whether life has actually been made more tolerable as a result of the intervention. Few hospital statistics even distinguish between discharge and death, let alone give any follow up link to subsequent morbidity and mortality data. According to Ferguson and MacPhail (1954) two years after leaving hospital 36.3 per cent of medical patients are dead and 56.6 per cent dead or 'unimproved.' All surgery, however minor, carries with it psychological costs to the patient and real risks to life. Few surgical procedures have had a balance of their costs and benefits investigated. One suspects that the risks associated with much common surgery compare unfavourably

96

with many drugs which have been banned on the grounds of risk.

Patients want and demand action when they are ill and doctors are anxious to give it to them. Although the evidence in favour of tonsillectomy is so frail and its recommendation is dependent upon fashion and subjective opinion, parents appear to queue to subject their children to the terror of being deserted in the company of total strangers in a foreign environment to await some unknown (at least to the child) fate. Malleson (1973) has pointed out that in New York the risks associated with child tonsillectomy are twelve fold greater than for a pregnant women having an abortion: to run the same degree of risk she would have had to have been on the pill for 160 years. Cochrane (1972) rightly contrasts the use of resources on tonsillectomy with the provision of hearing aids to the elderly. One is widespread but dubious with a positive risk; the other effective, riskless, but unfashionable and under provided. There are probably about one million elderly people who would benefit if they were sought out and aided.

The ideal would be if all medical intervention were deemed useless until positively shown to be otherwise. Certainly enthusiastic and often brilliant work is already being done in this direction but the backlog is enormous. Randomised clinical trials to discover what difference, if any, a given form of intervention makes has been widely advocated by Cochrane and increasingly put into practice. Cost-benefit analysis to discover whether this difference is both positive and worthwhile is also under way. Thus increasingly a range of important questions are being asked:

a)   to intervene or not?
b)   which treatment to intervene with?
c)   where should the intervention take place?
d)   for how long?
e)   what priority does the intervention take?

These questions are not exhaustive but they are the most crucial. Of course, the problems are enormous even when the soul is willing. It should be fairly straightforward to determine whether treatment 'A' prolongs or shortens life, but the quality of that life may be of equal importance. How do we weight one year of perfect mobility against five years of serious disability (Culyer, 1971)? These are mainly problems for the future, however, as much current practice may well be shown to have little or no effect on either life expectancy or its quality. There is, of course, also the complication that a placebo will often produce a positive effect and so treatments have to be compared with these, rather than with total inaction.

Cost effectiveness studies are most straightforward when the benefits are positive and identical. Even in this event, however, costs may outweigh the benefits for all forms of intervention indicating that none should, therefore, be adopted. A good example of a cost effectiveness study is that by Piachaud and Weddell (1972) who investigated two methods of treating varicose veins — injection-compression sclerotherapy and surgery. They assumed the medical outcome (benefit) from each treatment to be identical and found the cost per patient treated to be £44.22 in the case of surgery but only £9.77 for injection-compression sclerotherapy which could be undertaken in outpatients departments. Further, the outpatient treatment took only thirty hours of patient time as against the one hundred hours associated with surgery and the patient needed only 6.4 days off work as against 31.3. Obviously estimating the actual costs of surgery presented some averaging problems with respect to indivisibilities, but with differences as large as these, it is doubtful whether methodological problems could significantly influence the conclusions. Their survey clearly showed that outpatient injection therapy was the 'better buy.'

Klarman, Francis and Rosenthal (Cooper and Culyer, 1973) also tackled the problem of variable costs in their (now classic) study of chronic renal failure. They allowed for some variation in benefit, on the basis of added life expectancy crudely adjusted for 'quality.' They assumed that one year of dialysis was equivalent to 0.75 of a year of transplant. Transplant proved to be by far the better buy.

David Pole (Hauser, 1972) looked at the time of treatment in a cost-benefit investigation of mass radiography as a preventive measure and discovered that even on the most favourable assumptions the costs were double the benefits. One of the variables most frequently absent from all such studies undertaken to date is the private cost incurred by the individual undergoing the medical intervention. An interesting exception to this is the Exeter Institute of Biometry's studies into the costs and benefits of hospital as against home confinement. One study is currently directed towards investigating the private cost to the family of these alternatives (A.J. Cooper, 1974).

A very critical self-examination of current practices and a ruthless pruning out of the ineffectual can, in the long run, be scarcely avoided. The process has already begun. John Todd (1974) has suggested a list of economies for immediate adoption by his colleagues. He advises that they stop admitting (a) walking patients for investigation, (b) diabetics for 'stabilisation,' (c) fat women for weight reduction, and start (a) discharging patients as soon as they can reasonably be looked after at home and (b) operating whenever possible on a day bed basis. Finances must be found as not only must the standards of caring be radically improved, but the sheer volume of the chronic and long term sick is likely to increase substantially, creating still further financial strain. According to Klein and Ashley (1972) on present trends by 1992, 93.7 per cent of nonmaternity beds available for women will be filled with old age pensioners and 73.5 per cent of those available for men. The cost implications are formidable.

Changes in Delivery

Probably the most important structural question to be asked is whether the accelerating trend of general practitioners towards health centres will reverse the tendency towards a predominantly hospital based health service. To some extent hospital domination has already been held at bay by the development of modern pharmaceuticals, many of which make hospitalisation no longer necessary. Official Treasury figures, however, show no signs of any marked switch away from the hospital to community based health provision and general medical services will probably remain more or less constant *per capita* and a falling proportion of NHS spending (Table 22).

Although health centres were an integral part of the original intentions of the founders of the NHS, only in recent years have they begun to operate in any numbers. In 1966 the hope was that there would be 284 in operation by 1976. In practice, there are already four hundred

TABLE 22 Projected health expenditure at 1973 prices. UK 1973-4 to 1977-8.

	73/74	74/75	75/76	76/77	77/78	1973/4 to 1977/8
Capital Expenditure						
Hospital and community Services	255	248	242	231	228	- 11
Family Practitioners	.2	.2	.2	0	0	- 0.2
Other Health Services	11	3	4	4	4	- 64
Local Authority Health Services	26	26	24	24	24	- 8
Total Capital Expenditure	292	275	270	259	256	- 12
Current Expenditure						
Hospital and Community Services	1625	1682	1739	1796	1857	+ 14
Family Practitioners	598	622	646	670	691	+ 16
Other Health Services	49	54	53	53	53	+ 8
Local Authority Health Services	169	174	179	183	188	+ 11
Total Current Expenditure	2441	2531	2617	2702	2789	+ 14
Total Capital and Current Expenditure	2733	2806	2887	2961	3045	+ 11
Personal Social Services						
Capital Expenditure	87	78	83	87	85	- 2
Current Expenditure	389	411	438	468	504	+ 30
Total Current and Capital Expenditure	476	489	521	555	589	+ 24

Source: *Public Expenditure to 1977-8*, HMSO, 1973, Cmnd. 5519.

centres open and at least another four hundred in the pipeline. Although this is impressive progress, the centres only house thirteen per cent of all general practitioners and the health centre building programme has been drastically cut back as part of the overall public spending economies in the face of general economic difficulties. Further, until April this year (1974), the centres were the responsibility of Local Authorities and doctors have joined them for a vast range of unrelated reasons. The result is that both the size and nature of these centres is highly variable and not part of any well thought out master plan. The Todd Report (1968) saw them as involving ideally twelve doctors under one roof, serving a population of thirty thousand. Sited at transport focal points, and in close proximity to the social service offices, these purpose built centres would offer efficient appointment systems, diagnostic equipment (thus cutting down referrals) and a range of ancillary staff. The doctor would suffer less professional and academic isolationism and be able to undertake a small degree of specialisation.

The Harvard Davis Report (1971), however, thought in terms of only five or six doctors and rejected specialisation in favour of the general practitioner becoming a 'specialist in primary care,' putting medicine more into the 'social context' and maintaining close links with hospital based doctors by means of consultant visits to the health centre. In practice the current average is indeed five doctors although the range is an incredible one to twenty-two. Some centres consist of several group practices sharing one set of premises, whilst others consist of one large group and so on. Already some of the hopes for these centres are being questioned. Apppointment systems are becoming barriers rather than aids. Receptionists are becoming more important than formerly, due to the impersonalisation and sheer formality of the receptionist's 'enquiries desk.' Although the centres are now formally under the NHS umbrella, conformity and central influence are not going to be easy to impose even if the will to do so were present.

Quite apart from the health centres, general practitioners are increasingly working in groups. In 1959, for example, thirty-one per cent worked single handed and two per cent in groups of six or more.

By 1971, however, the respective percentages were twenty per cent and six per cent.

It may be that as doctors work together increasingly in large groups and as medical manpower shortages are increasingly felt to be acute, more attention will be given to using their time more effectively. In the USA the substitution of medical auxiliaries for doctors has already gone some way towards economising upon medical time. A recent study suggested that at least ten per cent of consultations used procedures well within the competence of a nurse and that over fifty per cent of the total time spent in consultations with the patient had no clinical component at all (Buchan and Richardson, 1974). A Canadian study was much less cautious. A nurse was shown to be able to handle over sixty per cent of all visits without the need to worry the doctor. Most importantly of all, she could handle a case load about half the size of that of the doctor and offer advice and reassurance with at least equal effect (Spitzer, 1974). None of this is surprising and yet in 1969 only forty-one per cent of a select sample of 576 doctors had direct access to the services of a nurse (Irvine and Jeffreys, 1971). In the same survey sixty-five per cent of the weighted total had no attached health visitor and seventy-four per cent no midwife. For doctors practising outside of groups, seventy-four per cent had neither a nurse nor a health visitor and eighty-four per cent no midwife.

Patients frequently want only advice and reassurance but there is the danger that due to the time constraint they may be given drugs. Doctors may be tempted to use Librium and Valium, for example, as effective ways of cutting a consultation short. Rather disturbingly, however, surveys show that as high as one third of all patients fail to take their prescribed drugs (Porter, 1969; Wilcox, 1965).

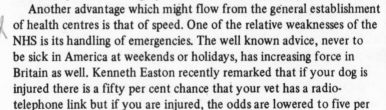

Another advantage which might flow from the general establishment of health centres is that of speed. One of the relative weaknesses of the NHS is its handling of emergencies. The well known advice, never to be sick in America at weekends or holidays, has increasing force in Britain as well. Kenneth Easton recently remarked that if your dog is injured there is a fifty per cent chance that your vet has a radio-telephone link but if you are injured, the odds are lowered to five per cent! Certainly large areas (South East England, South Wales and

Scotland) are largely without any immediate care facilities. Could not health centres remain open around the clock for emergency and minor accident work and the ambulance system made into a radio linked mobile emergency treatment centre? Clearly this is potentially the subject of an urgently needed cost-benefit study. It seems that doctors arrive at coronary cases on average four hours after the beginning of symptoms, but by this time fifty per cent of patients are dead (Partridge, 1967).

If even a small part of the hopes for a move towards 'community health teams' based upon health centres becomes a reality, the general practitioner is going to have to assume new roles. The profession has never in the past shown any natural inclination to merge with other professional groups as equals, and yet many 'cases' have social and medical problems so intertwined that they cannot be sensibly separated out. This problem has been particularly acute in the profession's relationship to social workers, who have refused to accept a subservient role, but medical claims of omnipotence are also being increasingly questioned within the hospital service by the post-Salmon nursing officers.

> 'In acute clinical situations there is no question, the doctor is the leader, but at other times — in slow restoration of the stroke patient or during convalescence — the nurse will frequently be the one most concerned with the patient's care and leadership may be considered to have passed to her, the doctor's role having become an advisory one.' (Skeet, 1974.)

Further pressure is growing for general practice nurses to be employed by the Area Health Authorities rather than by individual doctors. According to one authority, if a general practitioner is the nurse's employer it 'destroys the autonomy which is fundamental to professional status' (J. Clark, 1974). Clearly one clinical freedom impinges upon another.

Changes in Patient Demands

With their greater educational attainment and experience of the NHS, it is probable that patients will increasingly demand more information of their medical advisors. Decisions will increasingly be shared. Doctors must be more frank as to the probability of any medical intervention leading to material change in the patient's condition. Medicine cannot do something for everything. Doctors and nurses must assume increasingly the role of active health educators.

For their part it seems possible that patients will turn more frequently to self-help from over the counter medicines. Many ethical drugs could safely be left to the discretion of the pharmacist, being certainly no more dangerous than aspirin, and possibly less so. The role of the pharmacist must be redefined, as his present position and professional future is, to say the least, perilous. The development of the branded medical speciality has made him closely resemble a highly skilled counter of pills.

On the hospital front one very encouraging sign of things to come is the recent appointment of a 'director of patient services' at the new Charing Cross Hospital and of a social psychologist to investigate patients' reactions to food, noise, comfort and complaints. Certainly with rising standards of living and a growing realisation that the health service is not a charitable trust to which one must be eternally grateful for anything, the caring aspects and standards of amenity are going to be severely tested. Public awareness of the conditions endured by the mentally handicapped will eventually increase the cost of these services substantially. In the 1930s people lived with, and expected to live with, such things as toothlessness. Indeed many diseases died with their victims, totally untreated. In the future, aspirations as to standards will inevitably take further steps forward. Contact lenses may well replace spectacles, routine medical screening become annual, home helps be automatically provided during sickness and so on. Treatment will be demanded for the '28 day misery,' baby blues, menopausal and similar discomforts. Jean Robinson in Oxford has already pointed out that a predominantly male medical profession has made light of these female ailments. As women live longer and are more prone to mental illnesses, they have also suffered most from the relatively mean provision of resources to the caring aspects of the NHS.

In terms of gross national product it is often not true that prevention is cheaper than cure but in terms of human suffering the case will, with the passage of time, look increasingly convincing. The use of preventive medicine in the USA, for example, is strongly correlated with income and education. In 1969, fifty per cent of Americans had a health checkup, twenty-nine per cent of them unassociated with any reported symptoms. Preventive medicine in Britain has suffered from being statistical rather than personal, from being long run rather than immediate and therefore from being postponable.

Science has to date made surprisingly little impact upon the diseases of old age. The increase in life expectancy at seventy since 1901 is only eleven months for males, whilst the corresponding increase at birth is twenty years and four months! What would be the cost implications of a slowing up in the ageing process or even its reversal? Similarly what would be the cost implications of a cure for cancer involving six months in hospital or a treatment costing several pounds a week for life? The future is likely to see the development and prescription of mood modifiers, pacifiers, comforters and memory aids. Transplants will become routine — only the brain and spinal cord defying the advance of science and technology.

Widespread and crippling diseases remain little touched — rheumatoid arthritis, the allergies, migraine and so on. There is likely to be growing pressure for the relief of every day tensions, indeed according to one authority 'it is likely that by 1990 nearly every individual will be taking psychotropic medicines either continuously or at intervals.' Indeed, already every tenth night's sleep is hypnotically induced (Dunlop, 1970) and nineteen per cent of all British women and nine per cent of men are taking tranquillisers during the course of any one year (Klerman, 1974). The control of aggression and antisocial behaviour is another possible growth point. Obesity may be fought by drugs rather than by eating less. Heart patients may even be able to monitor their own rhythms and take appropriate action when they detect a disturbance. Finally as many diseases become rarer, 'natural immunity' may diminish creating new demands for vaccines (Teeling-

Smith, 1970).

All in all, demands are likely to increase rapidly in the immediate future. Thresholds of tolerance of pain, discomfort and poor amenities are continually lowering. Further there appears to be an unmistakable trend towards the individual taking less and less responsibility for his own health state. A neglected, ill-treated body is going to give trouble sooner or later. Individuals need to be taught and encouraged to take care of their own health states. At present, however, health education expenditure amounts to less than 0.01 per cent of the NHS's expenditure.

9 CONCLUSIONS

It is inevitable that in a short book the emphasis should be upon what has been wrong rather than upon what has been right. It is important therefore to stress that in the opinion of this writer the NHS compares favourably with all other known systems. Inequalities of treatment, inefficiencies and the maldistribution of resources are found world-wide. In the USA, affluent areas are well doctored but many areas, such as the Upper Midwest, fail to attract any primary care practitioners at all. Professional birth control keeps salaries high and preserves a large medically deprived population intact. Resources are duplicated in some areas and denied to others and, whilst the fashionable branches of medicine flourish, others founder. This book in no way supports the view that the NHS needs to be dismantled, rather it is a plea for still closer scrutiny of its problems and for the zealous protection of its many virtues.

The health service was founded upon a basic misconception of the nature of the need for health care resources. The concept of sickness as an unambiguous and absolute state led to the false hope that unmet need could be abolished. In practice sickness has been found to be a relative state capable of almost infinite interpretation by both patients and the medical professions. There has proved to be no allocation of national resources which would eliminate the necessity for the health service to ration its services amongst competing claims upon them.

The process by which final demands upon the service are determined is complex and certainly involves many non-medical considerations which remain only poorly understood. What emerges as certain is that demand tends to outstrip supply. Rationing, however, has never been explicitly organised but has hidden behind each doctor's clinical freedom to act solely in the interests of his patient. Any conflict of interest between patients has been implicitly resolved by the doctor's judgements as to their relative need for care and attention. The clinical freedom to differ widely as to their conception of need has led to inconsistencies of treatment between patients and to the allocation, without challenge, of scarce resources to medical practices of no proven value.

Within the NHS there has been no one with the position and authority to denounce the incompetent, to censure the idle and to monitor the health and fitness of medical colleagues. Such a situation is particularly unhappy in the hospital context where the patient has to place himself trustingly and completely in the hands of a total stranger whom he has had no hand in selecting. Complaints involving clinical judgement have traditionally met with the response 'shut up or sue.' The new Health Service Commissioner, Sir Alan Marre, who is a kind of final Court of Appeal, is specifically excluded from investigating 'any action taken in the course of diagnosis, treatment or clinical care which, in the commissioner's opinion, was taken solely in the exercise of clinical judgement' (DHSS, 1972 (a), p. 56). Clinical freedom can become an excuse for clinical licence. Gross variations in medical practices have been defended on the grounds that standardisation and uniformity would impede progress and reduce the opportunity for experimentation. There has been in practice, however, little systematic use made of variations and no one would in any case suggest a regimentation which excluded conscious research and experimentation.

At the very least, such clinical freedom from criticism and guidance suggests regular relicensing. It could be argued that doctors should not be allowed such freedom to practice based mainly upon a performance in examinations which may have taken place thirty or more years in the past. The aircrews of passenger air services are given Ministry approved checks every thirteen months. Cabin crews are given yearly survival and emergency checks. Are surgeons really any less susceptible to obsolescence, sickness or incompetence?

The NHS tacitly accepted that the activities of doctors were outside of managerial control. Management has decided what resources should be made available at each level, whilst doctors have been left free to decide their best deployment. In practice, of course, these are inseparable. For their part, the Central Department has been content to

108

delegate responsibility downwards so that even long term plans have reflected the sum of regional hopes and aspirations. The lack of research into indicators of need has enabled gross inequalities of provision to persist on the grounds that, in the absence of any evidence to the contrary, they might in fact, however accidentally, reflect needs. Further, the nature of need has enabled the service to continuously claim shortages of manpower and other resources. It has remained easier to demand more of the taxpayer than to critically reexamine current practices and to prune out waste.

Shortage, within the context of an administered market, can only mean a shortfall from some technically defined ideal. It may well be that such an ideal is itself a constant function of actual provision and unobtainable. Certainly, any claim for more resources must be seen in the light of competing claims. A well founded case is necessary, but not sufficient, grounds for obtaining more resources. Such a case must follow, and not precede, a careful scrutiny of current practices and deployment of resources.

One of the most apparent needs in the health service is for more information of all kinds, at all levels. Regular flows of tailored data are required, for example, on resources available by locality and speciality, usage patterns and the variables that determine them, unmet needs, the evaluation of treatment and so on. Doctors need to know if they differ from their colleagues; the service needs to know why. Statistics gathered to make up tables in the *Annual Report* are not enough. Of course, information is not a free good and needs itself to be justified on cost-benefit principles. Hopefully the new administrative structure, aided by the computer, will bring great improvements in these aspects of the NHS.

Although the NHS has greatly increased both the potential and actual demand for health care, in practice it has been forced to ration supply by means which in their own way are almost as ruthless (but generally held to be more acceptable) as the ability to pay. This book has tried to pose the question as to whether, with a better understanding of need and with a reappraisal of the nature of clinical freedom, unavoidable rationing would not take place more rationally, consistently and efficiently to the mutual benefit of taxpayer and patient.

BIBLIOGRAPHY

B. Abel-Smith and K. Gale (1964), *British Doctors at Home and Abroad*, Codicote Press.

J. Ashford and N.G. Pearson (1970), 'Who uses Health Services and Why?', *Journal of the Royal Statistical Society*, 133, 3, Series A.

Michael Alison (1972), personal communication.

Michael Alison (1973), *Hansard*. Vol. 859, 9 July, col. 1225.

J.M. Bevan and G.J Draper (1967), *Appointment Systems in General Practice*, Oxford.

P. Bierman (1968), *Milbank Memorial Fund Quarterly Review*, 46, 77.

E.R. Bransby (1973), 'Mental Illness and Psychiatric Services,' *Social Trends*, No. 4, HMSO.

R. Briggs (1974), 'Supply of Blood Clotting Factor VIII', *Lancet*, 1, 1339.

J.H.F. Brotherston (1970), in W. Lathem and A. Newberry (eds), *Community Medicine: Teaching, Research and Health Care*, Butterworth.

C.V. Brown (1968), 'Misconceptions about Income Tax and Incentives', *Scottish Journal of Political Economy*, February.

R.G.S. Brown (1973), *The Changing National Health Service*, Routledge and Kegan Paul.

J.C. Buchan and I.M. Richardson (1974), *Time Study of Consultations in General Practice*, Scottish Home and Health Department.

J. Bunker (1974), 'Risks and Benefits of Surgery', in *Benefits and Risks in Medical Care*, OHE.

J.S. Bulman, N.D. Richards, G.L. Slack and A.J. Willcocks (1968), *Demand and Need for Dental Care*, Nuffield Provincial Hospitals Trust, Oxford.

J.R. Butler, J.M. Bevan and R.C. Taylor (1973), *Family Doctors and Public Policy*, Routledge and Kegan Paul.

J.R. Butler and M. Pearson (1970), *Who Goes Home?*, Bell.

A. Cartwright (1964), *Human Relations and Hospital Care*, Routledge and Kegan Paul.

A. Cartwright (1967), *Patients and their Doctors*, Routledge and Kegan Paul.

T.E. Chester (1973), 'Health Service Reorganised', *National Westminster Bank Review*, November.

J. Clark (1974), 'Bring Nurses into the GP fold', *Pulse*, 14 September.

A.L. Cochrane (1972), *Effectiveness and Efficiency: Random Reflections in the Health Services*, Nuffield Provincial Hospitals Trust, Oxford.

A.L. Cochrane (1971) in W.A. Laing (ed), *Evaluation in the Health Services*, OHE.

D.R. Cook (1972), 'The Reorganisation of the NHS – Viewpoint of the GP', *Journal of the Royal Society of Health*, 92, 1.

A.J. Cooper (–), *The Private Costs of Maternity Care*, M.A. Thesis.

M.H. Cooper (1974), 'The Economics of Need: The Experience of the British National Health Service' in M. Perlman (ed), *The Economics of Health and Medical Care*, Macmillan.

M.H. Cooper (1971), 'How to Pay for the Health Service', *Journal of the Royal Society of Health*, Vol. 91, No. 5.

M.H. Cooper (1966), *Prices and Profits in the Pharmaceutical Industry*, Pergamon.

M.H. Cooper and A.J. Cooper (1972), *International Price Comparison*, NEDO.

M.H. Cooper (1974), *Social Policy*, Blackwells.

M.H. Cooper (1974), 'Financing and Rationing Health Care Resources', in W.D. Reekie and N. Hunt, *Management in the Safety and Social Services*, Tavistock Press.

M.H. Cooper and A.J. Culyer (1970), 'An Economic Analysis of Some Aspects of the NHS', in I. Jones (ed), *Health Services Financing*, BMA.

M.H. Cooper and A.J. Culyer (1972), 'Equality in the NHS: Intentions, Performance and Problems in Evaluation', in M. Hauser (ed), *The Economics of Medical Care*, Allen and Unwin.

M.H. Cooper and A.J. Culyer (1972), 'An Economic Survey of the Nature and Intent of the British NHS', *Social Science and Medicine*, Vol. 5, No. 1.

111

M.H. Cooper and A.J. Culyer (1968), *The Price of Blood*, IEA.

M.H. Cooper and A.J. Culyer (1974), 'The Economics of Giving and Selling Blood', in A. Seldon (ed), *The Economics of Charity*, IEA.

M.H. Cooper and A.J. Culyer (1973), *The Pharmaceutical Industry in the United Kingdom*, Dun and Bradstreet.

D.L. Crombie and K.W. Cross (1959), 'Serious Illness in Hospital and at Home', *The Medical Press*, 242, 316, 340.

D.L. Crombie (1974), 'Morbidity Statistics from General Practice', in *Risks and Uncertainty in Medical Care*, OHE.

Richard Crossman (1969), Reported in the *Guardian*, 27 November.

Richard Crossman (1972), *A Politician's View of Health Service Planning*, University of Glasgow.

A.J. Culyer (1973), *The Economics of Social Policy*, Martin Robertson.

A.J. Culyer, A. Williams and R.J. Lavers (1971), 'Health Indicators', *Social Trends*, HMSO.

A.J. Culyer and J.G. Cullis (1973), 'Hospital Waiting Lists', *New Society*, 16 August.

G.I.B. Da Costa *et al* (1974), *Hospital Medical Staffing*, Hospital Consultants and Specialists Association.

Dan Mason Nursing Research Committee (1970), *Home From Hospital*, quoted in R.G.S. Brown (1973).

R. Doll (1973), 'Monitoring the NHS', *Proceedings of the Royal Society of Medicine*, 66, 729.

R. Dollery (1971) in *Challenges for Change*, (ed) G. McLachlan, Nuffield Provincial Hospitals Trust, Oxford.

Y. Dror (1968), *Public Policy Making Reexamined*, San Francisco Chandler Pub.

D.M. Dunlop (1970), 'The use and abuse of psychotropic drugs', *Proceedings of the Royal Society of Medicine*, 63, 1279.

D.M. Dunlop and R.S. Inch (1972), 'Variations in Pharmaceutical and Medical Practice in Europe', *BMJ*, 23 September.

K. Dunnell and A. Cartwright (1972), *Medicine Takers, Prescribers and Hoarders*, Routledge and Kegan Paul.

A. Eardley and J. Wakefield (1974), *What Patients Think about the Christie Hospital*, University Hospital of South Manchester.

C.P. Elliott-Binns (1973), *Journal of the Royal College of General Practitioners*, 23, 255.

A. Engel and P. Siderius (1970), 'The Consumption of Drugs', *WHO Chronicle*, 24, 68.

M.S. Feldstein (1967), *Economic Analysis for Health Service Efficiency*, North Holland.

T. Ferguson and A.N. MacPhail (1954), *Hospital and Community*, Nuffield Provincial Hospitals Trust, Oxford.

G. Forsyth and R.F.L. Logan (1968), *Gateway or Dividing Line*, Nuffield Provincial Hospitals Trust, Oxford.

G. Forsyth (1973) in *Health Service Prospects*, (eds I. Douglas-Wilson and G. McLachlan), Lancet and Nuffield Provincial Hospitals Trust, Oxford.

G. Forsyth and R.F.L. Logan (1960), *Demand for Health Care*, Nuffield Provincial Hospitals Trust, Oxford.

G. Forsyth (1966), *Doctors and State Medicine*, Pitman Medical.

G. Forsyth (1967), 'Is the Health Service doing its Job?', *New Society*, 19 October.

John Fry (1972), 'Twenty-one years of General Practice', *Journal of The Royal College of General Practitioners*, 22, 121.

John Fry (1966), *Profiles of Disease*, Livingstone, Edinburgh.

John Fry (1974), *Self Care: Its Place in the Total Health Care System*, The Panel on Self Care.

O. Gish (1971), *Doctor Migration and World Health*, Bell.

Mary Green (1974), 'A fairer deal for the nurses', *Daily Telegraph*, 4 May 1974.

P. Harrison (1974), 'Compulsory Psychiatry', *New Society*, 16 May.

J.T. Hart (1971), 'The Inverse Care Law', *Lancet*, i, 405.

S.C. Hayward (1974), *Managing the Health Service*, Allen and Unwin.

M.A. Heasman (1964), *Lancet*, 2.

J. Horder and L. Horder (1954), *The Practitioner*, 173, 177.

R. Hinchliffe (1961), 'Prevalence of the commoner ear, nose and throat conditions in the adult male population of GB', *British Journal of Preventive Medicine*, 15, 3, 128.

B. Hunter (1972), *The Administration of Hospital Wards*, University of Manchester.

I. Illich (1974), 'Medical Nemesis', *Lancet*, 1, 918.

Institute of Hospital Administrators (1963), *Hospital Waiting Lists*, London.

D. Irvine and M. Jeffreys (1971), 'BMA Planning Unit Survey of General Practice', *BMJ*, 4, 535.

S. Israel and G. Teeling-Smith (1967), 'The Submerged Iceberg of Sickness in Society', *Social and Economic Administration*, 1, 1.

K. Joseph (1973), *Daily Telegraph*, 30 June.

N. Kessel and M. Shepherd (1965), 'The Health Attitudes of People who seldom consult a Doctor', *Medical Care*, III, 6.

King Edward's Hospital Fund (1973), *Accounting for Health*, King Edward's Fund.

H.E. Klarman, E. Herbert, J.O.S. Francis and G. Rosenthal (1968), 'Cost Effectiveness Analysis applied to the Treatment of Chronic Renal Disease', *Medical Care*, Vol. 6, 48.

R. Klein (1974), 'Policy Making in the NHS', *Political Studies*, XXII, 1.

R. Klein and J. Ashley (1972), 'Old Age Health', *New Society*, 6 January.

R. Klein (1971), 'Mismanaging the NHS', *Management Today*, December.

R. Klein (1973), 'An Anatomy of the NHS', *New Society*, 28 June.

R. Klein *et al* (1974), *Social Policy and Public Expenditure*, Centre for Studies in Social Policy.

G.L. Klerman (1974), 'Social Values and the Consumption of Psychotropic Medicine', *Proceedings of the 1st World Congress of Environmental Medicine and Biology*, North Holland

J.M. Last (1969), 'Community Demand for Doctors in the next Ten Years', *BMJ*, 5646, 769.

J.M. Last (1967), 'Objective measurement of quality in general practice', *Supplement to the Annals of GP (Australia)*, Vol. XII, 2.

W. Laing (ed), *Evaluation in the Health Services*, OHE.

R.J. Lavers and M. Rees (1972), 'The distinction award system in England and Wales', in *Problems and Progress in Medical Care*, Oxford.

D.S. Lees and M.H. Cooper (1963), 'Research into General Practice', *Journal of the College of General Practitioners*, 6, 3, 233.

D.S. Lees and M.H. Cooper (1963), 'The Work of the General Practitioner', *Journal of the College of General Practitioners*, 6, 4, 408.

D.S. Lees (1965), 'Health through Choice', reprinted in *Freedom or Free-for-All*, (ed. R. Harris), IEA.

S. Lichtner and M. Pflanz (1971), 'Appendectomy in the Federal Republic of Germany: Epidemiology and Medical Care Patterns', *Medical Care*, ix, 311.

R.F.L. Logan, J.S.A. Ashley, R.E. Klein and D.M. Robson (1972), *Dynamics of Medical Care: the Liverpool Study into the use of Hospital Resources*, LSHTM.

W.P.D. Logan and E. Brooke (1957), *Survey of Sickness 1943-51*, HMSO.

C. McCreadie (1974), 'Reviews', *Social Policy*, No. 1, 89.

J.M. Mackintosh, T. McKeown and F.N. Garratt (1961), *Lancet*, 815.

A. Malleson (1973), *Need your Doctor be so Useless?*, Allen and Unwin.

H.G. Mather (1971), 'Acute myocardial infarcation: Home and Hospital Treatment', *BMJ*, 3, 334.

G.K. Matthew (1971) in *Portfolio for Health*, G. McLaughlin (ed), Nuffield Provincial Hospitals Trust, Oxford.

R. Maxwell (1974), *Health Care: The Growing Dilemma*, McKinsey.

Medical Research Council (1966), *Lancet*, ii, 997.

H. Miller (1973), *Medicine and Society*, Oxford.

D. Morris, A. Ward and A.J. Hendyside (1968), 'Early Discharge after Hernia Repair', *Lancet*, 681.

Nuffield Provincial Hospitals Trust (1960), *Casualty Services and their Setting*, Oxford.

Office of Health Economics (1974), *The Work of Primary Medical Care*, London.

Office of Health Economics (1965), *The Cost of Medical Care*, London.

Office of Health Economics (1967), *Progress in Mental Health*, London.

Office of Health Economics (1963), *Hospital Costs in Perspective*, London.

Office of Health Economics (1967), *Efficiency in the Hospital Service*, London.

Office of Health Economics (1966), *Medical Manpower*, London.

Office of Health Economics (1964), *The Costs of Medical Care*, London.

Office of Health Economics (1965), *Work Lost Through Sickness*, London.

Office of Health Economics (1971), *Off Sick*, London.

Office of Health Economics (1970), *Building for Health*, London.

Office of Health Economics (1971), *Prospects for Health*, London.

Office of Health Economics (1972), *Hospital Purchasing*, London.

Office of Health Economics (1972), *Medicine and Society*, London.

Office of Health Economics (1974), *The NHS Reorganisation*, London.

D. Paige and K. Jones (1966), *Health and the Welfare Services in Britain in 1975*, Cambridge.

J.F. Partridge and J.S. Geddes (1967), 'A mobile intensive care unit in the management of myocardial infarction', *Lancet*, ii, 271.

D. Piachaud and J.M. Weddel (1972), 'Economics of treating varicose veins', *International Journal of Epidemiology*, i, 3.

J.D. Pole (1972), 'The Economics of Mass Radiography' in *The Economics of Medical Care*, M. Hauser (ed), Allen and Unwin.

Political and Economic Planning (1961), *Family Needs and the Social Services*, Allen and Unwin.

Political and Economic Planning (1944), *Medical Care for Citizens*.

A.M. Porter (1969), 'Drug Defaulting in a General Practice', *BMJ*, i, 218.

E. Powell (1966), *Medicine and Politics*, Pitman.

E. Powell (1962), 'Health and Wealth', *Proceedings of the Royal Society of Medicine*.

Pulse (1974), 23 March.

A.M. Rees (1972), 'Access to the Personal Health and Welfare Services', *Social and Economic Administration*, 6, 218.

I.M. Richardson *et al* (1973), 'A Study of General Practice Consultations in N.E. Scotland', *Journal of the Royal College of General Practitioners*, 23, 132.

B. Robb (1967), *Sans Everything*, Nelson.

D. Robinson (1971), *The Process of Becoming Ill*, Routledge and Kegan Paul.

K. Robinson (1966), *Hansard*, V. 740, col. 1559.

K.J. Roghmann and R.J. Haggerty (1972), 'The Diary as a Research Instrument in the Study of Health and Sickness Behaviour', *Medical Care*, X, 142.

D.L. Rosenham (1973), *Science*, 20 January.

R. Rowbottom (1973), *Hospital Organisation*, Heineman.

Royal College of General Practitioners (1973), *Present and Future Needs of General Practice*, Royal College.

Royal College of General Practitioners (1973), *Morbidity Statistics from General Practice*, second National Survey.

Royal College of General Practitioners (1968), *Reports from General Practice*, VIII, S.W. England.

Royal College of General Practitioners (1965), *Reports from General Practice*, II, Present State and Future Needs.

R. Scott and M. Gilmore (1966), 'The Edinburgh Hospitals', in G. McLaughlan (ed), *Problems and Progress in Medical Care*, Oxford University Press.

J. Seale (1962), *BMJ*, i, 782.

A. Seldon (1967), 'National or Personal Health Services', *Lancet*, 1.

J.T. Shuval (1972), 'The Sick Role in a Setting of Comprehensive Care', *Medical Care*, X, 50.

Muriel Skeet (Chief Nursing Officer of the British Red Cross) (1974), quoted in *Pulse*, 4 May.

R. Stevens (1966), *Medical Practice in Modern England*, Yale.

P.J. Taylor (1968), 'Personality Factors Associated with Sickness Absence', *British Journal of Industrial Medicine*, 25, 105.

G. Teeling-Smith (ed) (1970), *Medicines in the 1990s*, OHE.

G. Teeling-Smith (1972), 'Health, Wealth and Happiness', *Social and Economic Administration*, 6, 135.

K.B. Thomas (1974), 'The Temporarily dependent patient in General Practice,' *BMJ*, 30 March.

R.M. Titmus (1963), *Essays on the Welfare State*, Allen and Unwin.

J.W. Todd (1974), *BMJ*, 31 August, pp. 577-8.

P. Townsend and D. Wedderburn (1965), *The Aged in the Welfare State*, Bell.

A. Vaarlem *et al* (1972), 'Patients' Opinions of their Doctors,' *Journal of the Royal College of General Practitioners*, 22, 811.

M.E.J. Wadsworth, R. Blaney and W.J.H. Butterfield (1971), *Health and Sickness: the Choice of Treatment*, Tavistock Press.

R. Weatherall (1964), *Proceedings of the Royal Society of Medicine*, 57, 1043.

P.A. West (1973), 'Allocation and Equity in the Public Sector: the Hospital Revenue Allocation Formula,' *Applied Economics*, 5, 3.

K.L. White, T.F. Williams and B.C. Greenberg (1961), 'The Ecology of Medical Care,' *New England Journal of Medicine*, 268, 885.

F.G. Whitehead (1971), 'Trends in Certificated Sickness Absence,' *Social Trends*, 2.

D.R.C. Wilcox, R. Gillan and E.H. Hare (1965), 'Do psychiatric outpatients take their drugs?', *BMJ*, 2, 709.

W.O. Williams (1970), 'Reports from General Practice No. 12,' *Journal of the Royal College of General Practitioners*.

D.C.L. Wroe (1973), 'The Elderly,' *Social Trends*, No. 4, HMSO.

Official Reports

Annual Reports of the Hospital Advisory Service, 1970 onwards; HMSO.

Central Health Services Council (1971), *Report on the Organisation of group Practice*, (Harvard Davis Report), HMSO.

DHSS (1970), *The Future Structure of the NHS*, HMSO.

DHSS (1972a), *NHS Reorganisation in England*, Cmnd. 5055, HMSO.

DHSS (1972b), *Management Arrangements for the Reorganisation of the NHS*, HMSO.

DHSS (1973), *Health and Personal Social Services Statistics for England (1973)*, HMSO.

DHSS (1972), *Report of the Chief Medical Officer of Health on the State of Public Health for 1971*, HMSO.

DHSS (1969), *The Functions of the District General Hospital*, (The Bonham-Carter Report), HMSO.

DHSS (1973), *Report of the Committee on Hospital Complaints Procedure*, (The Davis Report), HMSO.

DHSS (1974), *Community Hospitals: their role and development in the NHS*, HMSO.

General Household Survey (1973), *Introductory Report*, Office of Population Censuses and Surveys, HMSO.

Ministry of Health (1956), *Report of the Committee of Enquiry into the Cost of the NHS*, (Guillebaud Report), Cmnd. 9663, HMSO.

Ministry of Health (1962), *Hospital Plan for England and Wales,* Cmnd. 1604, HMSO.

Royal Commission on Medical Education (1968) (Todd Report), Cmnd. 3569, HMSO.

Report of the Committee on Nursing (1972), (Briggs Report), Cmnd. 5115, HMSO.

Report of the Committee on Senior Nursing Staff Structure (1966), (Salmon Report), HMSO.

Report on confidential inquiries into maternal deaths in England and Wales 1967-9, (1972), HMSO.

Report on an enquiry into maternal deaths in Scotland 1965-71, (1974), HMSO.

Report of the Expenditure Committee, (1971), (Employment and Social Services Sub-Committee), Minutes of Evidence 31 March 1971 and 21 April 1971, HMSO.

Report on Social Insurance and Allied Services, (1942), (Beveridge Report), Cmnd. 6404, HMSO.

Report of the Committee of Enquiry into Allegations of Ill Treatment of Patients and Other Irregularities at Ely Hospital, Cardiff, (1969), (Howe Report), Cmnd. 3975, HMSO.

Report of the Farleigh Hospital Committee of Enquiry, (1971), (Watkins Report), Cmnd. 4557, HMSO.

Report of the Committee of Enquiry into Whittingham Hospital, (1972), (Payne Report), Cmnd. 4861, HMSO.

Report of the Committee of Enquiry into South Ockenham Hospital, (1974), (Hampden Inskip Report), Cmnd. XXXX, HMSO.

Report of the Expenditure Committee, (1972), Eight Report, HMSO.

Report of the Joint Working Party on the Organisation of Medical Work in Hospitals, (1974), HMSO.

Report of the Committee to Consider Future Numbers of Medical Practitioners and the Appropriate Intake of Medical Students, (1957), (The Willink Report), HMSO.

Report on the Control of Public Expenditure, (1961), (The Plowden Report), Cmnd. 1432, HMSO.

Select Committee on Procedure (1969) Session 1968/9, HC 410, HMSO.

Social Trends, Nos. 1 to 4, 1970-3, HMSO.

World Health Organisation (1969), *World Health Statistics,* Vol. III, UN.

INDEX

Abortion, 12, 97.
Accident departments, 54, 103.
'Aches and pains,' 11.
Adequacy, concept, 25, 26, 27, 41-5.
Adenoids, removal, 55.
Administration: staff, 36; structure, 72-81, 109.
Aircrews, relicencing, 108
Alcoholism, 19, 46.
Allergies, 105.
Ambulance service, 93, 103.
Anaemia, 13.
Anaesthetics, 80.
Analgesics, 12.
Ancillary medical staff, 101, 102.
Appendicitis: bed rest, 55; mortality, 57-8.
Appointment systems: barriers, 101; general practice, 53, 54; health centres, 101; out-patient departments, 94.
Area Health Authorities, 76, 77, 78, 103.
Armstrong, Sir William, 26.
Ashford, John, 54.
Ashley, J., 99.
Aspirin, 104.
Audit: groups, 59; stock, 70.

'Baby blues,' 104.
Ballot box, 8, 50.
Barrow, admission rates, 55.
Beds: allocation to consultants, 72; availability, 22, 68; average daily use, 18; bed rest, 58, 70, 80; distribution, 40, 66; and the need formula, 71; numbers, 36.
Bermondsey, sickness, 11.
Bevan, Aneurin, 25.
Beveridge, Sir William, 25.
Birmingham: hospitals, 55; merit awards, 63; region, 63.
Blood pressure, 13.

Blood sugar, 20.
Blood Transfusion Service, 77, 80.
Bonham Carter Report, 41.
Brain tumours, 14.
Briggs, Rosemary, 92.
British Medical Association: Advisory Panel on Health Service Financing, 82, 83-84; Conference of Local Medical Committees, 43; Representative Body, 43; *Journal*, 43.
British Rail, facilities, 41, 94.
Bristol heart disease, 57.
Bronchitis, 13, 55.
Brown, C.V., 83.
Butler, J.R., 62.

Cabinet, 27.
Canada: import of doctors, 39; use of medical auxiliaries, 102.
Cancer, 14, 57, 105.
Capital expenditures, 25, 26, 32, 40-1, 43, 60, 63, 77, 99-101.
Capitation payments, 18, 61.
Carstairs, V., 56.
Cartwright, Ann, 11, 15, 94.
Casualty departments, 54.
Catering, 66, 68.
Charges, user, 9, 82, 83-4, 89, 90.
Charing Cross Hospital, 104.
Children, 21, 77, 92, 93, 97.
Chloramphenicol, 22.
Cholagogues, 22.
Christie Cancer Hospital, 95.
Chronically sick, 28, 38, 84, 96, 99.
Clinical freedom, 9, 53, 56, 57, 58, 59, 71, 72, 80, 90, 95, 103, 107-8, 109.
Cochrane, A.L., 97.
Coefficient of correlation, 63.
Coefficient of variation, 64.
Cogwheel committees, 79, 80.
Common cold, 13.